P9-CAL-745

# CLASSROOMS THAT WORK

## A TEACHER'S GUIDE TO

# DISCIPLINE WITHOUT STRESS

## STAN SHAPIRO & KAREN SKINULIS
## with RICHARD SKINULIS

Published by Practical Parenting Inc., Toronto

Copyright © 2000 by Stanley Shapiro, Karen Skinulis.

All rights reserved. No part of this publication may be reproduced or transmitted in any form or by any means, electronic or mechanical, including photocopying, recording, or by any information storage and retrieval system, without permission in writing from the publisher.

Practical Parenting Program Inc.
250 Harding Blvd. W., P.O. Box 32142
Richmond Hill ON L4C 9S3
Tel: 905-770-0606 Fax: 905-770-4836
parent@interlog.com
Toll free 1-877-210-0593

Distributed in the United States by
Practical Parenting and Classrooms Program
119 Schilling Lane
Rochester, New York 14618
parent@interlog.com
Toll free 1-877-210-0593

Cataloguing in Publication Data
Shapiro, Stanley.
Classrooms That Work: A Teacher's Guide to Discipline without Stress

ISBN 0-9681352-9-3

Classroom Discipline. Skinulis, Karen.
Skinulis, Richard.
Title.

Cover and text design by Christine Higdon

**Other Works by the Authors**

*Parent Talk: 50 Quick, Effective Solutions to the Most Common Parenting Challenges.* Toronto: General Distribution Services Limited, 1997.

*Practical Parenting: A Common Sense Guide to Raising Cooperative, Self-Reliant and Loving Children.* Toronto: Practical Parenting Program Inc., 1996.

Printed and bound in Canada

# CONTENTS

## ACKNOWLEDGEMENTS

We would like to thank the following people for their help in writing this book:

Sheila Shapiro, for always being there to do what had to be done. Christine Higdon, for creating such beautiful designs. Corey Finkelstein, for the web site, flyers and other design work. Maria Gonzolaz for the excellent copy editing and suggestions. Alex McCombs, for sharing his wonderful teaching techniques with us. We would also like to thank all teachers everywhere, who have taken on the task of leading our children to the unlimited possibilities of the future.

# PREFACE

The impetus for this book came from my experiences as a school psychologist, in the classroom teaching children and later, leading workshops for teachers and parents. I was struck by how much children wanted to learn and how strongly teachers wanted to teach. The trouble was, the largely authoritarian system they all had to function in had flaws that prevented them from doing either.

My epiphany occurred when I met renowned child psychologist Rudolf Dreikurs in 1965. His revolutionary approach to understanding children and their behavior set in motion a life long interest. The concepts he espoused – things like democratic methods, encouragement, consequences, and class meetings – opened up exciting new directions. I have been using these techniques for over 35 years. I have seen how they can turn children on to education while improving the relationships with their teachers. I know that they work. I know they will work for you.

My co-author (who also happens to be my daughter) and myself have tried to back up the theoretical aspect of the book with very practical techniques that will easily put the theories to use. To accomplish this, nothing is more practical than the class meeting, something a large part of the book is taken up with. Learning how to conduct these meetings on a regular basis, as well as how to include your students in them, is the key to having a disciplined classroom that is truly free from stress.

I deeply believe that if teachers understand and embrace these ideas, if they have respect for their students and trust in the possibility of their cooperation, it can not only change the classroom but the way we prepare our children to face the challenges of the adult world.

*Stanley Shapiro*
Richmond Hill, Ontario
November, 2000

# CHAPTER 1

# The classroom in transition

The one unalterable fact about our present era is constant and relentless change. Fortunately, change always opens the door to opportunity. We are now presented with an opportunity to help finish the work that the entire 20th Century was about – the struggle for equality. All the great events and movements of the last 100 years: the victory of the democracies over fascism in World War II, universal suffrage, the civil rights and feminist movements; and the drive for equal treatment for the physically and mentally challenged, are all about the shift from authoritarian rule to democratic ideals and social equality. The only identifiable group in our culture that has yet to be fully included in this concept of equality is our children. But that is changing too. It began in the early 60s with pioneers such as Dr. Benjamin Spock and Rudolf Dreikurs, and continues today with the plethora of parenting and child-rearing books and programs we are witnessing. We are moving from a time when adults were considered superior to children and child rearing strategies followed the autocratic formula that had been in place for centuries, to one in which democratic ideals are becoming accepted.

One of the fault lines where these old and new theories of child rearing meet is in the classroom. Teachers are struggling to find appropriate, meaningful and constructive ways of establishing relationships with their students, while maintaining discipline in the classroom within this new and evolving context. The concepts and strategies contained in this book are a proven way to do just that. But to understand where we are going we must also take a look at where we are coming from.

Let's look at a teacher in a mid-century classroom. Fifty years ago the world was a more sedate place where things changed at a much slower rate, which gave at least the illusion of stability. In that world, discipline was universal. Almost everyone – teachers, principals and parents – agreed on the way to handle discipline problems, which was through the judicious application of punishments and rewards. Teachers ruled with a leather strap in the drawer and a ready smile for their favorite students. There were common problems of behavior back then of course, but nothing like the ones faced by today's teachers. Here are some words and concepts that had yet to appear in the teacher's list of concerns as recently as 1950:

- drugs
- gangs
- guns
- eating disorders
- video games
- computer addiction
- school shootings
- high divorce rates
- latchkey kids
- materialism
- ozone depletion
- AIDS
- species extinction
- political correctness
- child pornography
- attention deficit disorder
- overtly sexual/violent entertainment
  (movies, music videos, etc.)

The last half of this century has experienced such an exponential growth and change that today's teacher operates in a radically different day-to-day reality. It's not that all of the changes have been bad – advances in technology and science have the potential to greatly help the human race – it's just that they come at us with such increasing speed and have such unsettling, stressful effects, many of which we don't even have time to comprehend. The unavoidable result for teachers is that they have an infinitely more complex, difficult and sensitive job. But what is much worse is that, while the world, the classroom and the students who make it up have changed, the techniques of maintaining discipline have not.

Same teacher, 21st century classroom: Styles of dress range (depending on the economic level of the school) from designer clothes and expensive running shoes to major league sports paraphernalia. Even young girls are wearing makeup. Both sexes follow fashion styles generated by media-driven celebrities. The different cliques in the classroom can be readily identified by their style of dress. The consumer society has worked so well that many students are more interested in getting the latest products then learning. The more subtle pleasures of the explorations of the mind have paled beside the instant gratification of the next purchase.

The desks are grouped together instead of in rows. Banks of computers line the walls. The students click through computer programs with practiced ease as the screens flash by at a dizzying speed. Some of the children have pagers and even cell phones to find out which of their parent's homes they will be sleeping at. In an increasing number of schools, there may be a breakfast program. Some of the students are being prescribed either antidepressants or stimulants, often because they have extreme behavior problems.

At noon the lunch boxes come out, having been packed that morning by busy parents just before they both rush off to work. A significant proportion of these students come from either single parent or blended families.

Depending on the school board, the parent group, and the individual teacher, the discipline style of today's classroom could be anything from a laissez-faire/permissive method to a strict, 50's style autocratic model, or a democratic approach based on mutual respect. The universality of discipline is gone, replaced with conflicting styles and experimentation. It's no wonder then that we are beginning to question things such as teacher accountability and parental involvement.

When teachers turn to the experts for the answers to these hard problems, the advice is often conflicting. Some advocate a return to authoritarian models, others advise moving towards democratic ideals. Obviously, society has still not fully committed to the idea that children are our social equals. Our position, and the reason we have written this book, is that by accepting children as social equals, we can not only motivate them to higher achievement, but actually improve cooperation and motivation in the classroom. This means that you can in fact establish good working relationships with your students while inspiring them to be happier, emotionally healthy children who are not only working up to their full potential but are also learning how to be caring people and good citizens as well.

# CHAPTER 2

# The new classroom: going democratic

Making the change from an autocratic to a democratic philosophy of discipline is bound to produce some feelings of dislocation. If you have been teaching for a number of years, it may not be easy to accept the changing roles of teacher and student. It may be even harder if you feel you have had some measure of success with the old method.

The first step is to look at some of the negative by-products of the autocratic (teacher-led) classroom and how they can work against realizing the full potential of your students, including their social skills and awareness of themselves and others.

Aside from learning the curriculum, the primary goal of an autocratic teacher is to achieve obedience. The students in this kind of classroom are expected to follow rules without question, turn to the teacher for solutions to all problems, seek approval and validation from authority, and in general to do the right thing in order to avoid punishment. Although you may end up with some obedient students, you unfortunately also sacrifice their initiative and problem solving skills. In other words they become passive, and as a result they are unconcerned about the welfare of others. Students who want to please or avoid trouble can become passive partly because they are accustomed to being told what to do, but also because they are not being asked to think about the group. For obvious reasons, being responsible only for yourself stifles social interest, which is a major catalyst for positive human attributes such as caring, compassion and social involvement. The autocratic system doesn't cultivate these ideals, instead, it produces followers who are taught to obey. The trouble with that is, obedience to someone else means you don't question or think for yourself.

Participatory (democratic) classrooms, on the other hand, are successful at teaching students to not only do the right thing in the classroom, but elsewhere, and for the rest of their lives, even when there is no one making them do so. It creates an atmosphere in which leaders, not followers are fashioned. Where children's energies, youthful enthusiasm, fresh thoughts and ideas can be fully nurtured and realized.

Another major drawback to the teacher-led class is the resentment it can cause. Any human being, regardless of age or social status, resents being told what to do or being made to conform. We might do it, but that doesn't mean we're happy about it. We are all (yourself included) much more apt to go along with a desired behavior when we have agreed to it. The trick, of course, is getting your students to agree to cooperate. The greater part of this book is devoted to helping you learn how to win that cooperation.

## The Five-minute test

Ultimately, the true test of a well-disciplined class is when you leave the room. If you can leave for five minutes and return to a well-functioning class, you're on the right track. This lets you know that your students have developed internal controls. Often with the autocratic method, the students rely on the teacher to provide the discipline – the reason to behave. When you're gone the discipline falls apart.

*Frances is a grade five teacher who rigidly controls her class using threats, detentions, and yelling in conjunction with treats, kind words, and stars for the "good" students. Enormous amounts of time and energy are spent keeping the children in line, but she is proud of how orderly her classroom is and will often boast: "You can walk into my class at any time and see quiet kids working away at their desks. "Frances is right, her classroom is orderly and well behaved – until she leaves the room. When she goes, the discipline goes right along with her because the discipline – the desire to cooperate – doesn't exist within her students. When she is gone, or a substitute teacher comes in, all hell breaks loose. The students take advantage of the fact that no one is there to control them. What is even more disturbing is that Frances has also been the victim of hurtful graffiti in the washrooms, the telltale sign that resentment is boiling just below the surface of her seemingly orderly classroom. At recess, when her students are let out from her classroom, they fight, argue, and run much wilder than the other children. Once again, when they are on their own with no one making them behave, they lack the internal checks to behave on their own.*

The real problem with the classroom that Frances is so proud of is that her students are not being given a chance to develop self-discipline. Frances may be able to get through the curriculum by the end of the year, but surely there is more to school than passing exams. Is obedience the only goal? Don't we also want children who have a good sense of inner responsibility, who can control their impulses and act well even when they are not under someone's thumb? Won't the traditional kind of short-term thinking cause them to become people who only work hard when someone makes them?

Another irony of the seemingly orderly teacher-led classroom is that, instead of saving time, it ultimately costs the teacher time because of the inordinate amount of surveillance and energy it takes to keep the pressure on. It is a system in which the students have made no investment. Constantly being controlled, they easily become resentful, and resentful people find it almost impossible to have good feelings about the person controlling them. The atmosphere in this kind of classroom can be poisoned by even one rebellious child.

*Kim is a grade eight student in an autocratic style classroom. He doesn't like being under his teacher's thumb, and plays the smart aleck a lot; a talent that has made him a hero to some of the other kids. He is an expert at getting very close to the line of unacceptable behavior and then pulling back. He seems to be saying: "You can make me be here, but you can't make me like it." Kim's teacher retaliates by giving him detentions and by humiliating him in front of others, while verbally patting the heads of the better-behaved students. Kim is growing to like his new role as class rebel and is exhilarated by the battle. His teacher, on the other side of the battle line, is becoming increasingly frustrated and exhausted by a battle he is beginning to feel he can't win. "If only I could reach this kid," he sighs to himself.*

Despite all of his teacher's efforts, Kim won't cooperate because the teacher's control methods are feeding into the power struggles and strengthening Kim's resolve to rebel.

Yet another problem with the teacher-led method is that it squanders the most powerful classroom management tool the teacher has at his or her disposal – the peer group.

The opinion of a child's peers is just as important, if not more so, than the teacher's. The teacher-led method, for the most part, ignores this powerful peer group pressure, except for when exerting its negative use in humiliating a child in front of others, or when creating competition. Our task is to find a way of using the peer group as a positive influence. As you will learn in the chapters ahead, the skillful use of tools such as sociometric tests, conflict resolution, communication skills, and class meetings, help to create an atmosphere where students not only help make the rules, but also help enforce them for the good of all. The results are greater social awareness, feelings of belonging and acceptance, and higher self-esteem.

## THE DIFFERENCE BETWEEN DEMOCRATIC AND PERMISSIVE

**PROBLEM:** "Isn't this really about giving the kids what they want and giving up a lot of my responsibility as a teacher?"

**ANSWER:** Don't mistake the democratic method for a permissive approach, which means not having clear rules and well established consequences for breaking them. This approach features a lack of consistency, in which the limits shift according to the teacher's mood. This kind of teaching style is by far the least effective. Unfortunately, in their desire to avoid being autocratic and to remain well liked, a lot of teachers become permissive. They try to win their student's approval by letting them do pretty much what they want.

Sharing power in the democratic method does not mean giving up your leadership and authority. In fact, respect for the teacher is high because students have been taught how to work well together without letting the misbehaving children get away with anything. That means a better-behaved class in the long run.

# CHAPTER 3

# Motivation from within

## Extrinsic motivation

At the heart of the autocratic approach to discipline is the concept of extrinsic motivation. This is the belief that one can get desired behavioral results in children by punishing the undesirable behavior and rewarding the good. Children, this philosophy goes, cannot be expected to do right unless they either fear punishment or hope for rewards. Everything from corporal punishment, humiliation and detentions to stickers, special privileges and candy, have been used to coerce and control students in this way. It is assumed that the desire to act appropriately has to come from outside rather than from within the child himself. This method forces us to think of the child as a piece of clay that can be shaped and formed by a carrot-and-stick approach.

*Jenna has forgotten her homework again. Fed up, her teacher makes her write out "I will not forget my homework" 100 times as punishment. With a scowl on her face, Jenna scrawls out the required lines. A week later, she forgets her homework again, this time getting 200 lines and a note sent home to her parents. Jenna's forgetfulness continues despite the punishment. That's because her teacher has not dealt with the inner motivation behind the problem – in this case, Jenna is resistant to demands made upon her time (a power goal that has shown up in other areas of Jenna's life). Despite the fact that she hates doing lines, this punishment will not work in her case because in her mind, every time she "forgets" her homework, she "wins."*

Punishments are ineffective when the child has dug in her heels (Goal Two, page 49) and takes on the teacher. In fact, the more punishments, anger, and control tactics used on Jenna, the more resistant she will become in order to prove that she can't be made to do what she doesn't want to do. Despite the punishment, she feels in control because the teacher has not defeated her.

*Troy is a seven-year-old boy who is having trouble reading. His teacher, along with the school program in place, has established a book tracking system that rewards the children who read the most books. Already discouraged, Troy's heart sinks as he looks at the prominently displayed list and sees that he has the fewest stickers next to his name. Realizing he can never catch up and in fact has already lost the race, Troy is less and less inclined to read while the top readers (already encouraged) reap all the rewards. At the same time, some of his classmates, in overreaction to the competition, have resorted to listing books they haven't read.*

Rewards are unnecessary for those already motivated and reinforce the discouragement of those that aren't. They also have the negative effect of encouraging cheating. Unfortunately, this approach is so ingrained in our thinking that it is truly difficult to imagine maintaining order in any other way.

The fact that children defeat us time and time again when we use rewards and punishment (external motivators) proves that the only real solution lies within the child themselves. We must find a way to turn on their internal motivation.

# Intrinsic motivation

Intrinsic motivation involves tapping into the child's own desire to do the right thing. It comes from within rather than from without. The teacher's challenge here is to flip the "on switch" connected to the child's intrinsic or built in desire to cooperate and work hard. Of course, this natural urge to act appropriately only occurs under the right circumstances, but when it is cultivated, there is no limit to the successes the child can experience. Her real potential will be realized because she truly wants to behave appropriately and apply herself to learning.

*Amanda, 12, is having trouble learning her multiplication tables. Overwhelmed, she feels math is too difficult for her and as a result, has not worked hard in this subject. By the seventh grade, all her classmates know their times tables and the teacher is no longer working on this skill. Like a lot of children, Amanda is ashamed of not knowing what everyone else knows and tries to hide her deficiency. Her teacher looks over her math test and points out that she knows what mathematical operations need to be done, even though she got the answer wrong. He avoids discouraging her by first pointing out her strength.*

*Teacher:* "Amanda, it looks like you do understand the process of the problem, you're just having trouble with the calculation."
*Amanda:* "I know. I studied for the test, but I can't seem to work out the right answers."
*Teacher:* "OK. Let's look at this problem you had trouble with. You got this first part right but ran into trouble here. You didn't get the multiplication right."
*Amanda:* "I guess I just made a mistake."
*Teacher:* "Maybe you did, but I also see the same problem cropping up in the next three questions."

*Amanda sullenly looks down at her hands and doesn't answer. She is obviously embarrassed.*

*Teacher:* "I can see this is bothering you. Can we talk about it?"

*Amanda: "Why bother? I just can't do this."*
*Teacher: "You sound as if you've already given up, as if there is no hope."*

*Amanda nods her head in agreement.*

*Teacher: "I know you find this very hard to do, but I also know that together we can solve this problem. It's certainly not too late, so don't worry about that. Let's come up with a plan together to help you catch up. The only area I see that you really need to catch up in is your times tables. I'd be happy to spend some extra time helping you. We won't stop until you are all caught up."*
*Amanda: "But I can never remember them. I've tried. Everyone else can, but not me. I'm the only one."*
*Teacher: "You believe you have a poor memory, but I know that you don't. You have a fantastic memory for social studies and science. You remember difficult ideas and express them very well. I know your ability to memorize things is very good because you have shown that in your other subjects. What do you think about what I just said?"*
*Amanda: "I never thought of it in that way. Maybe you're right. What should I do now?"*
*Teacher: "Let's start with this and see how we do."*

*Her teacher begins with a simple task he knows she will be successful at. He takes out three multiplication flash cards and asks her to study them for a moment. They go through them easily. She makes one mistake, they go over it again, and she gets them all right this time.*

*Teacher: (looking at his watch) "It only took you five minutes to learn these three problems. We'll stay with them for this week, and each week build on this solid base you have created today. Let's set up a schedule so we can work on this. Can you come in again?"*
*Amanda: "I guess so."*
*Teacher: (with enthusiasm) "Learning these tables will make a world of difference to your math – you'll see. I'll be here to help you."*

Amanda and her teacher have agreed on a plan of action, and Amanda leaves the meeting with some hope, whereas before the meeting she had none. The teacher's task is to continue the support and encouragement that will change the child's belief from "I can't do this" to "I can." As long as the child continues to feel that there is hope, she will start to want to work, and feel a sense of accomplishment when she does. There is no better alternative for this kind of problem. Punishments and rewards will only exacerbate the child's feeling of discouragement.

# CHAPTER 4

# The encouraging teacher

*"Encouragement is more important than any other aspect of child raising. It is so important that the lack of it can be considered the basic cause for misbehavior. A misbehaving child is a discouraged child."*

– RUDOLF DREIKURS, CHILDREN: THE CHALLENGE

The main source of discouragement for children in a classroom is the feeling that the work is too difficult. The student may feel she's not capable, that she can't do it, that she is stupid, in other words, a failure. She may be angry with herself or at other people, such as the teacher who is giving her the work that is overwhelming her. She may also be anxious – about taking tests, about looking incompetent in front of her friends and being ostracized from the group. She may, in fact, have given up hope of ever handling the material.

Your task as a teacher is to motivate this discouraged child to move towards overcoming all of these negative and self-defeating attitudes. You can best accomplish this by being encouraging.

Encouragement engenders a belief that one is capable, and that one's contribution is important. Some people are naturally encouraging. In their company, you just feel good about yourself. Others need to learn how to be encouraging. It's a skill like any other that can be broken down into parts and learned. The first step in becoming an encouraging teacher is to learn how to encourage yourself. You can do this by first accepting that nobody is perfect and that we all make mistakes. If you lose your temper with your students, say to yourself: "That was ineffective. It may have let off steam, but it didn't help my students learn what I wanted to teach them. Next time I will be more effective."

The essence of encouragement is to focus on a child's strengths, on what's "right" with the child, not on weaknesses, or what's "wrong." Even if you make a mistake in an encouraging classroom, you are encouraged to try again. Every effort is made to find something positive in the mistake itself. This gives courage to the child – the courage to take a chance and try something even if they don't know what the outcome will be. It gives them, in other words, the courage to fail.

If something is a bit of a reach for them and they fail, let them know it was a good effort and that you know they will eventually succeed. All the while, remind yourself that mistakes are part of life and that failure is not a catastrophe unless we make it so. The point to understand here is that it is important to work for improvement, rather than perfection. Try and set up expectations and goals the child can actually attain. Let your students know that his efforts are more important than the results and that it is more important to try than to succeed. After all, learning is often a process in which we fail at something but continue on until we get it right. Your job is to instill in your students the idea that it is okay to fail, that it is a part of learning. We often underestimate children. Showing that we have faith lets them know that we trust them and have confidence in them even when they are less than successful.

But encouragement is more than just building up the individual. It also has to do with stimulating someone to reach beyond themselves and become concerned and caring about the wellbeing of others. Some people have argued that the greatest happiness and contentment a human being can feel occurs when they know they have contributed to someone else's happiness (see Social Interest, page 101). For this reason, the art of encouraging students must also involve giving them opportunities to help and contribute to the wellbeing of the class. Find opportunities to allow children to be of service to someone else, such as helping each other find a lost article, assisting a younger student in a subject they are not strong in, or consoling an upset friend. You can also try to identify responsibilities you are currently doing that your students could do instead.

Here are some comments that encourage social interest:

- ✎ "Doing that was very helpful."
- ✎ "I appreciate your thoughtfulness."
- ✎ "We couldn't have done that without you."

## Encouraging statements

As with most things in life, it's the little things that have the most impact. This is doubly true when dealing with a discouraged student. In order to coax the child into believing she can do it, start by pointing out the little improvements in her work, even to the point of overemphasizing. In doing this it's very important to catch her at the moment of effort, and then to be very enthusiastic.

Use phrases like these to point out even minute attempts:

- ✎ "Boy, you're really keeping at it. You're not giving up."
- ✎ "You're determined."
- ✎ Say to him: "You may feel that you can't do it, but I'm confident that you are very capable. That's because I've seen it in other things you have done." You then point out the other areas that he has triumphed in, especially if he had experienced some trouble at first.

Here are some more examples of encouraging statements that can be used in almost any circumstance. Notice that they can be used both when the child has done something wonderful and when they have made a mistake. Also keep in mind that in order for encouraging remarks to have a positive effect, you must let them know that you really do believe they can do it. Tone is also important. A preachy, patronizing tone will not work, even if the words are encouraging. These encouraging statements are good at stimulating effort, developing cooperation and showing appreciation for work done:

- ✎ "You really seem to enjoy doing that."
- ✎ "It would be a great help to me (us) if you could do this particular job."
- ✎ "You are really getting much better at doing that."
- ✎ "Don't give up. Keep trying."
- ✎ "I'm sure you can figure out a solution to this problem."
- ✎ "I like the way you handled that."
- ✎ "I know you want us to think you can't do that, but we think you can."
- ✎ "If you need help, you know where to find me."

The following encouraging statements demonstrate acceptance and caring to your students:

- ✎ "I enjoy teaching you."
- ✎ "I'm glad to see you."
- ✎ "We missed you while you were sick."
- ✎ "I hear that you were helpful and cooperative – you did a good job."
- ✎ "I appreciate your help, your ideas, and your support."
- ✎ "I love the colors you used in this picture."
- ✎ "I like that idea."
- ✎ "I love your drawing, painting."
- ✎ "I enjoy talking to you."
- ✎ "I know you can do it."
- ✎ "Knowing you, you'll really pull this off."

## The practical aspects of encouragement

You can encourage your students by:

- ✎ Letting them know you have faith in them.
- ✎ Working for improvement rather than perfection.
- ✎ Treating all mistakes as learning opportunities.
- ✎ Stressing that efforts are more important than results; that it is more important to try than to succeed.

Encouraging comments and strategies from the teacher are essential, but we must also tap into another resource – the peer group. Getting the rest of the class to join in further increases the impact on the discouraged student. That's because children trust their peers more than adults. They often feel that the adults may be exaggerating or buttering them up, but they feel their peers are more honest. Also, they strongly want to be accepted by the group. What you want is for the student's peer group to tell her she's smart and capable; that she can do it.

# Encouraging exercises

Here are some activities you can try with your class to foster peer encouragement.

### Strength bombardment

This one can be done after the class knows each other fairly well. Form into groups of six. The group bombards each person in their group (one at a time) with all of the strengths they see in them. The person being bombarded is to remain silent. One person writes down all the strengths and then gives the person the list when it is over. There should be at least 10 strengths on each list and only positive statements should be made.

### Success sharing

Each person in the class is to share one event in their life that they are the most proud of – some kind of personal success that made them feel particularly good. There are three parts to this exercise:

- ✎ Tell everyone about the event.
- ✎ Tell them why it was important to you.
- ✎ Tell them how you felt about it.

Another variation on this theme is to wait until the end of the day and have each student share one thing they succeeded at or learned during the day. If they can't think of anything (those with low self-esteem may even think they are incapable of success at anything) you or others in the class can point out some for them. In fact, kids are usually more generous than we give them credit for, and will often volunteer successes for a student who can't think of anything for themselves. These reports can also be written if you are trying to build up their writing skills. Along with being encouraging, this exercise strengthens students' understanding that they are learning something in school, and that it is worthwhile.

*(The following two exercises were suggested by Jack Canfield and Harold C. Wells in* 100 Ways to Enhance Self-Concept in the Classroom.*)*

## The magic box

This one is perfect for younger students. Decorate a box and put a mirror on the inside opposite an open end. Ask your class who they think the most special person in the world might be. Then tell your class that you have come across a magic box that reveals to anyone who looks into it who the most special person in the world is. Put the box in another room and tell each student to go in one by one and look inside, stressing that they must keep what they see a secret for now. After they have all looked inside, ask them to tell the class who the magic box said was the most special person. After each one has had a chance to say "me," explain that the power of the magic box is that it teaches us that we are all very special. In order to encourage a discussion about uniqueness, you can then ask the class how they think it is possible that everyone is the most special or important person in the world.

## The pride line

Each student stands up and begins a sentence with "I am proud of..." and then goes on to tell the class about something they have done or can do that they are proud of. If they have trouble getting started, you can suggest something, such as "I want you to tell the class how proud you are about your math skills." If someone doesn't want to do it, let them pass.

Here are some suggestions:

- ✎ Things you've done for your parents.
- ✎ Things you have done for your siblings.
- ✎ Something you have made.
- ✎ Something you have done to fight racism.
- ✎ Money you have raised for a good cause.
- ✎ Temptations you have avoided.
- ✎ How you earned some money.
- ✎ How you helped someone else.
- ✎ A skill you have cultivated.

## WORDS TO TEACH BY

Praise is a verbal reward that evaluates the person.

Encouragement evaluates the deed, not the doer.

Pampering involves constantly doing for children what they could do for themselves, and sheltering them from all unpleasantness. This can lead to lack of self-confidence.

# Discouragement

Anything we do or say that lowers a person's self-evaluation of their character, abilities, degree of competency or even their general worth, is discouragement.

A discouraging approach treats all mistakes as "bad," which makes the child fearful of making mistakes and unwilling to try anything new. Discouragement concentrates on the child's weaknesses and lowers self-esteem. It is the direct opposite of being encouraging. Constant criticism, correction, and judgment are the hallmarks of the discouraging approach.

Finding fault is easy. Unfortunately, North America is a fault-finding culture, so it comes naturally to us (think of this the next time you mark all the wrong answers on a test with big red Xs). This reinforces our belief that if we point out what someone is doing wrong, they will correct it and not make the mistake again. But the truth is just the opposite – criticism lowers self-esteem and actually makes it harder for children to improve. Of course, anyone with very high self-esteem can handle a little criticism. These children can take critical remarks in their stride. However, most children get more criticism than they can handle, and at that point it becomes discouraging. Reflect on how you feel when someone criticizes you. Then think how a child feels when you criticize them.

Don't feel that every single mistake has to be pointed out and corrected. It may be hard to hold back the correction when a young student makes a mistake in verb tense, such as when they say something like, "That's the mostest I ever saw." But you must remember that children will eventually learn it themselves by modeling the correct usage by adults. Constant criticism has the opposite effect of what is intended, and will slow down the learning process as the child feels less and less capable. If you find you are giving out one encouragement to every ten criticisms (which is common), you should reverse the ratio, or even eliminate the critical remarks altogether.

Remember, encouragement is an ongoing process, so it's

important to keep it up. One critical remark can undo a week's worth of encouraging ones. In an encouraging atmosphere, people feel free to be themselves because they don't have to be so careful about what they do or say. This feeling of freedom and acceptance leads to a feeling of overall wellbeing.

## Discouraging statements

Here are some examples of discouraging statements:

- ✎ "Don't spill that."
- ✎ "I think you could have done a better job of that."
- ✎ "Your friend Jacob could have completed that."
- ✎ "Oh no! You did it again."
- ✎ "Here, let me do that for you."
- ✎ "You're too young to do that."
- ✎ "Don't get dirty."
- ✎ "Don't be late."
- ✎ "You could do that if you weren't so lazy."
- ✎ "I thought I could trust you."

## Praise

It's always a surprise for teachers to hear that praise is not the same as encouragement. Praise (which is part of extrinsic motivation) is a positive evaluation from the person who has superior status to one that has inferior status. Praise is never given to a social equal. Encouragement, on the other hand, is not a final evaluation but is recognition of a person's effort. Think of your best friend who has done something nice for you. You may thank the friend and tell them how much it helped you, but you would never tell them how good (or smart, or kind or pretty) they are because of what they had done for you. To avoid this mistake, use the same kind of encouraging statements you would say to your best friend.

Perhaps the biggest problem with praise is the dependency it can create. In fact, some children who are given a great deal of praise can become addicted to it. They wait for it after every thing they do and can become upset or unsure of themselves when it doesn't happen. But we don't want children to become dependent on the evaluations of others to make them feel they are okay. We want them to find this conviction from within themselves.

Praise is also a problem because it evaluates the whole person rather than the deed. When a child is successful, we might tell him how smart he is in math. It feels good to hear this "nice" label, but it may lead to worries about "what if I fail the next math test?" It follows then that if he makes a mistake or fails a test, he feels he is no longer smart. However, neither is correct. It only means that when he did well, he understood the concept and when he didn't do well he didn't understand the concept. Albert Einstein failed arithmetic in fourth grade. Does that mean he was a poor mathematician? People have a tendency to label the person with their achievement or their lack of it. We all have the potential to do well in most any area if we don't give up, and we tend to give up when we put a negative label on ourselves – "I'm no good at this." Praise is also problematic because it can only be used when the child has been successful. This can cause stress or anxiety because the child knows he won't get the praise next time if he doesn't pull it off. Encouragement, on the other hand, can be used at any time, even if the attempt is less than successful, which is when the child needs it the most.

Another problem with praise, especially if you go overboard with enthusiasm, is that the child may feel manipulated – that you are buttering them up in order to get them to act in a particular way. If the child has any self doubts at all he may not believe you. He may also think: "That's not true, because you don't really know me."

## Pampering

Pampering is a greatly misunderstood phenomenon and often not even recognized as one of the root causes of the problems teachers face in the classroom. It involves many things, including:

- ✎ Doing things for children that they are developmentally ready to do for themselves.
- ✎ Giving them undue attention.
- ✎ Letting them have an overabundance of things – toys, clothes, music, videos, and entertainment in general.
- ✎ Always giving them their own way.

The trouble with pampering is that it creates an expectation, and a "me first" attitude that can hinder the development of social interest and cooperation. That's because the pampered child is not encouraged to do for others or to think about others. In fact, famed psychiatrist Alfred Adler identified pampering as one of the most discouraging influences on a child.

The pampered child will appear less independent than her peers, more demanding, less patient, unenthusiastic about having to work, uncomfortable with the give-and-take nature of the playground, and often angry when her demands aren't met. She may express the idea that "things aren't fair."

Some of your students will come from pampering homes. These parents pamper because they want to insulate their children from obstacles, frustrations and painful situations. They may suffer from a deep lack of trust in their child's capabilities, and don't believe their children can handle these difficult or stressful things. Another major reason for pampering is that parents want to make their children happy, to see the momentary smile on their faces. To do this they try to anticipate every want and need of the child. It can also be done to make things easy for the overworked or harried parent. At the end of a long day, they don't feel energetic enough to be firm, so they give in and there is no immediate problem. Other parents take on all the responsibility because they believe that childhood should be a time of play – children can learn how to do things later. Ironically, they feel they are being especially good parents because they do so much for their children.

Pampering can also come from giving too much attention to a child. When this kind of child starts school and has to compete with 30 other children for the teacher's attention, he is unprepared to function independently.

More and more today we find that pampering comes in the form of children getting too much – treats, movies, videos, games, parties, toys, etc., – so much so that the boring, day-to-day job of learning can't compete. This is a big problem with today's consumer culture. When Maria Montessori founded her first classroom in the slums of Rome, the children were fascinated with the teaching materials, partly because they had so little else in their lives. We are not arguing that children be purposely deprived or under-stimulated, just that it's equally not good to keep them in a constant state of heightened excitement and entertainment.

Like other forms of discouragement, pampering leads to feelings of not being competent, lack of social interest, dependency, and even anger. It can make the child doubt his capabilities because he hasn't been given the opportunity to hone his skills. If someone is always doing things for you, you might expect this to happen continuously. Then there is disappointment when this doesn't happen. They can also feel overwhelmed when others expect them to pitch in.

Pampered children don't learn how to deal with their own frustrations. They make a demand and expect to get it right away. They never learn to develop problem-solving skills because someone is always there to solve problems for them. Consequently, they aren't ready to take on the focus, concentration, and hard work that learning requires.

School is one of the first organized social situations children encounter that is beyond their immediate family. It is the first place where they have to function in a group. Pampering inhibits their ability to cooperate with the group and focus on work. A pampered child could very well reach the early grades of school emotionally unready and find the demands of the classroom overwhelming.

## What can teachers do about it?

Fortunately, one of the best antidotes to pampering is the structure and group activity that the classroom provides. That's because it's not likely that the child will be pampered in the classroom environment. She is expected to work and to produce things that might not have been expected at home. Also, children in groups see that everyone is expected to work, which makes it easier to make the switch from being demanding to being cooperative. In other words, just being in the classroom will help a pampered child.

Specifically, teachers of pampered children should:

- ✎ Encourage independence.
- ✎ Be positive about the child's abilities and build up their confidence and desire to learn.
- ✎ Give them opportunities to solve problems, especially in classroom meeting situations.
- ✎ Provide firmness (remember, the child wants you to continue the pampering. Don't give in to their demands).
- ✎ Deal with their anger constructively by using problem-solving skills (see chapter 13) and the class meeting.
- ✎ Build up social interest by giving them responsibilities for others, i.e., everything from delivering messages to helping a fellow student with a tough subject and settling disputes.
- ✎ Help parents learn about the dangers of pampering. We know some teachers who regularly put together information sheets on interesting parenting topics – which could include pampering – and hand them out to parents. Sometimes the parents are unaware they are doing it, or that it is even a problem.

As a teacher, you should be aware that you could be pampering as well. As we all know, children are adept at getting service and attention and their own way by behaving as if they can't do things on their own. Often they are convinced that they really can't do it. While being "firm and friendly," point out that you know they can do it.

## High expectations and perfectionism

*"(Today's parents) are looking for winners.*
*They're looking for their kids to be the best in all things.*
*There's very little tolerance for normalcy."*
— DAWN WALKER, EXECUTIVE DIRECTOR OF THE
CANADIAN INSTITUTE OF CHILD HEALTH

Parents are becoming so concerned about their children's ability to compete and succeed in today's world that they are attempting to raise what amounts to "super kids" who can out-perform everyone else. Being good is often no longer good enough, you have to be the best. The problem with espousing heightened competitive ideals is that it takes the focus off of the joy of participation and the love of learning itself. It ignores the process and concentrates only on being number one. Since not everyone can be number one, this can result in a lot of unhappy children. A recent study by the Canadian Institute of Child Health, which followed 23,700 children from birth on, found that only 26% of the girls and 35% of the boys in grade 10 described themselves as being "very happy" about their lives. One of the conclusions about this result was that the high-pressured atmosphere of today's lifestyle may be leading teens to this result.

When we push our children too much, when our expectations are too high for them to attain, we set them up for failure. Of course this does not mean that children should not be taught to do their best. Obviously, we live in a competitive world where everyone must strive hard to succeed. But what has to be guarded against is the kind of mindless competition that is fostered so well by the "we're number 1" ethos of sports, as well as the

## THE PERFECTIONIST

Perfectionism is not so much an issue of competition as it is about meeting your own high ideals. The perfectionist is someone who feels they must achieve their ideal and if they don't, they aren't good enough. Everyone is imperfect, but the perfectionist is trying to be more than human; they are trying to be super human. Perfectionists tend to be: highly sensitive to criticism; less spontaneous than average; easily embarrassed by their mistakes; often very critical of others; focused on details; never satisfied, even after great accomplishments; and susceptible to eating disorders.

destructive and counterproductive competition that can easily be set up within families by comparing siblings to each other ("Your brother can do that better than you. Let's see if you can beat him."). Schools reinforce this at their very core by being based on a grading system and by giving out numerous awards, which ultimately leads to comparisons between students. The result is that the high achievers will be highly motivated and will attain what they go after. Unfortunately, the other children (the overwhelming majority) who see these goals as unattainable will often not try, and be beset by jealousy and feelings that the process is unfair. Ultimately, standards that are too high send the message that so much of what we do is just not good enough.

But how do we know when the bar has been raised too high and when it has not been raised high enough? Look at it this way, striving to do your best – your personal best – is both an enjoyable and effective way to spur yourself on. You can tell that this is happening when the students jump into an activity with enthusiasm. That tells you that they believe the goals you have set are attainable and are therefore motivating rather than discouraging.

## THE ATTRIBUTES OF
## A WELL-ROUNDED CHILD

▼ loves herself
▼ enjoys life
▼ is able to have fun
▼ has courage
▼ learns through mistakes
▼ is creative
▼ doesn't blame others
▼ enjoys people
▼ enjoys learning
▼ loves others
▼ sees the positive in people
▼ accepts challenges
▼ is optimistic
▼ does not have to be perfect
▼ is not self-critical
▼ cares about our environment
▼ eats properly
▼ has empathy for others
▼ is not fearful
▼ doesn't worry unnecessarily
▼ is not afraid to try
▼ takes responsibility for others
▼ enjoys giving to others
▼ continually moves towards self-reliance
▼ is interested in being healthy

## How to de-emphasize competition:

✎ Don't make comparisons ("Cecile got an A on this report. Why didn't you?").

✎ Don't be a fault-finder. People are always making mistakes.

✎ If you constantly point out mistakes without pointing out strengths as well, the student will feel he just can't do it.

✎ Stress cooperation over competition.

✎ Teach good sportsmanship in competitive situations, and practice what you preach.

## The Laziness myth

Surprisingly, what you might consider a "lazy" child is often in fact an over-ambitious child. It works this way: If the child buys into the credo that you have to be the best in order to just be okay, they are immediately in a high stress situation. They worry about losing face, status, and special privileges by not being good enough. The overly ambitious child who tries her best but comes in second may decide to not try at all. She may retreat to a safety zone where no effort is made. If a big exam comes up, her reasoning may be that if she doesn't study and doesn't do well, she has a ready-made excuse. "Of course I got a bad mark, I didn't study." If she manages to pull off a decent mark it's even more impressive because she did it without hard work.

To sum up, an encouraging teacher:

✎ shows enthusiasm

✎ has confidence and faith in his students

✎ recognizes the efforts of students

✎ sees the humor in situations

✎ notices and remarks on child's improvement

✎ emphasizes the child's strengths and assets

# OBSTACLES TO HIGH SELF-ESTEEM:

▼ spoiling and pampering
▼ neglect
▼ rejection
▼ no affection
▼ overprotection
▼ criticism
▼ finding faults
▼ physical and psychological punishment
▼ name calling
▼ pity
▼ domination
▼ having unreasonably high expectations

# CHAPTER 5

# "Why did they just do that?" Understanding misbehavior

## Unlocking the mystery of misbehavior

Teachers are often baffled as to why a child will repeatedly do something he knows is wrong. The fact is, children themselves often don't have a good understanding of their own behavior. When asked why they won't come in when the bell rings, for example, their answer is often a very honest "I don't know." That's because the mistaken goals of misbehavior are unconscious. Bringing these mistaken goals to light provides the teacher with a powerful tool to help understand why students act the way they do.

### Finding Significance

We are all social beings and our behavior can only be understood in a social context. All inappropriate behavior is an attempt by a discouraged child to find significance, as well as their place in the group. In the past, children were allotted more opportunity to make a real contribution to the family and society as a whole. Larger families, rural settings, and less technology meant that children were needed to help households and farms run smoothly. Today, except for schoolwork and extra-curricular activities, the role of children has been narrowed to that of playing and being entertained. It is much more difficult for children to feel they can make a real contribution and therefore develop social interest and feelings of significance. On top of that, discouraging atmospheres (at home or in the school) can diminish feelings of being accepted, appreciated, loved, and valued. The result is that a lot of children who have not been able to find a way to make a contribution in their social group fall into misbehavior with the mistaken idea that this will provide them with the significance they feel they are lacking. In a general sense then, we can say that all misbehavior is the child's attempt to find significance. Instead of trying to be helpful and make a positive contribution to the social group, children may attempt to fit in by reaching goals that elevate their own status rather than contributing to the group. After observing thousands of children, Rudolf Dreikurs did a wonderful job of categorizing the four mistaken goals that children strive for.

# The four mistaken goals of misbehavior:

*Goal One:* Undue Attention Seeking
*Goal Two:* Power
*Goal Three:* Revenge
*Goal Four:* Assumed Inadequacy

## Diagnosing

Diagnosing uncooperative behavior is as important in teaching as getting the correct diagnosis from your doctor when dealing with a medical problem. If every time a patient came to a doctor complaining of a headache and the doctor merely prescribed a pain reliever, she would be missing countless other possible causes and their treatments. Diagnosing your student's mistaken goal is the first step in correcting the problem.

To diagnose, first observe the student's behavior in detail. Pay attention to your own reactions, your own feelings and thoughts. Take notes if necessary. Then observe their reaction after you have corrected their behavior.

There are three steps to help make an accurate diagnosis:

*Step # 1 –*   How do you feel when the child is misbe-
              having?

*Step # 2 –*   What are your thoughts when the child is
              misbehaving

*Step # 3 –*   What does the child do when you intervene?

This three-step technique will be used in the diagnosis section following the discussion of each of the four goals.

# Goal One: The mistaken goal of undue attention seeking

The child that seeks undue attention feels significant only when she is the centre of interest. She enjoys it when people speak or notice her, even if they are yelling and upset. She doesn't feel she counts if she perceives herself as being ignored or forgotten. People usually think that the underlying cause for this is that the child didn't get enough attention, and sometimes this can happen when the child is neglected. A much more common cause, however, is that the child received too much attention when very young, or only got attention when she acted up. When a young child gets showered with attention, she becomes used to having people talk to her and entertain her all the time. When this is not happening, even for a short time, she feels uncomfortable and attempts to regain the spotlight. The key payoff for this child is the attention and service she receives, and she will get it in sometimes phenomenally creative ways.

# The four ways to seek attention

## 1. Active/Constructive:

High achievers that do wonderful things, but only in order to achieve recognition and praise, and not to learn or to help. The confusing part about this behavior is that it is, on the surface at least, socially useful and helpful. You can spot it because they constantly bring their accomplishments to your attention and demand a response. "Look teacher, I cleaned up the milk that Susan spilled!" Often followed shortly by "Look. I just drew a picture for you." If they aren't fed a steady diet of praise and recognition, however, the goodness stops.

## 2. Passive/Constructive:

These children don't use achievements to call attention to themselves, but instead use their personality. They are sweet, or funny, or make bright observations. They want to be recognized for their charm and wit. The typical teacher's pet. They don't so much do the right thing as say the right thing.

## 3. Active/Destructive:

The class clown, the show off, the mischief-maker, "macho man" or "super man." This child is going to do something – by asking questions, breaking rules, being exaggeratedly incompetent, making jokes or just generally running amok – to disturb the class and therefore call attention to himself.

## 4. Passive/Destructive:

The lazy kid who isn't going to do anything. He gets attention by obtaining service. He accomplishes this by being incompetent. His characteristics are: shyness, being frightened easily, dawdling, not wanting to perform, not willing to talk, and sloppiness.

Keep in mind that all children need and deserve a certain amount of attention. Sometimes, as when a child is behind in a subject, he really does need a lot more help. It is only considered undue attention when the needs of the situation don't call for it.

The mistaken idea of this goal is that he thinks the only time he counts is when someone is paying attention to him. This shows a dependency on others.

## Strategies for dealing with undue attention getting

*Omar is a bright, articulate boy. He often will walk into the classroom and immediately approach the teacher, who is talking to someone else, and interrupt with an urgent question. If you look closely, you will see that the question is in fact not so urgent and is something Omar could have figured out for himself. He then starts to talk with great gusto and animation with one of his classmates until the teacher is compelled to tell him to settle down and get to work. Omar peppers the day with small interruptions and disturbances – all fairly innocuous in themselves, but adding up to a lot of attention being paid to him.*

You can best deal with Omar by giving him less attention while encouraging him to be independent. Of course, you must keep in mind that needing and wanting social interaction is natural. It is important, therefore, for the child to learn how to belong to the classroom group through more constructive channels that result in closer relationships with group members.

It's important to realize that whenever a child is successful in getting undue attention from a particular behavior, he will likely repeat it because he has attained his psychological goal. The general strategy comes in two steps: step one is to not reinforce the misbehavior by giving the child attention when he demands it; step two involves giving extra attention when the child is acting in a cooperative, appropriate way. As their attention-getting mechanisms shift away from uncooperative to cooperative behavior, gradually wean them off of the attention altogether. You do this by building self-esteem, nurturing social interest, and helping children feel they belong without always being in the limelight.

There are several ways to ignore this misbehavior.

1. Mentally tune the child out. Don't feel you have to react to everything a child does, especially if it's a small thing, such as interrupting your conversation, endless questions, tapping a pencil on a desk, or pretending they can't do something you know they can. You don't always have to correct, criticize, nag, or answer. Sometimes the passive stance is best, particularly when the child's actions aren't infringing on someone else's right.

2. Ask the child to leave the room. This is used when the child is infringing on the rights of others, such as when clowning around, refusing to settle down so the class can get to work, or pestering others. Ask her to leave the room until she feels she can stop causing a disturbance.

3. Use proximity. You can walk over to where they are acting up and stand by them, without looking or talking to them, while still continuing with your lesson.

4. Give them a look without speaking. This will give them a certain amount of attention but not as much as they would like, while not disturbing the rest of the class.

5. Natural and logical consequences work well for undue attention. For example, by refusing to give extra service, such as helping the child in getting dressed for recess when he can do it himself, he misses part of recess. A lot of attention getters don't listen because they want to be given instructions separately. By refusing to repeat yourself, they miss out on important information.

Be warned that the misbehavior could escalate after you begin withdrawing attention. The good news is that it means you are on the right track because the child is just redoubling his efforts to get you to react the way you used to. If there is no payoff, the behavior will end over time. Look for positive behaviors you can give attention for that will make the child feel good about himself.

## Behaviors that say "Pay attention to me!"

- tattling
- shyness
- talking loudly
- dawdling
- asking a lot of questions (without waiting for the answer)
- chattiness
- talking too softly
- dressing inappropriately
- messiness
- helplessness

## Diagnosing undue attention seeking

1. What does the child do when you intervene? Given the attention that he seeks, the child will stop, either entirely or just momentarily, because he has achieved his goal.
2. What do you feel when the child misbehaves? You may feel annoyed and irritated when the child is trying to be the centre of attention.
3. What are you thinking during the misbehavior? Your thoughts may be along the lines of "What a pest."

## The Go and Stop signals

This is a good strategy for dealing with children whose goal is either attention or power.

We first saw this strategy when we were visiting an Adlerian school in Florida. As we sat in the back observing the class, we would see children standing up and walking out of the room periodically. This would happen up to ten times in one hour. We were puzzled, but later learned that they had been given a "go signal" by the teacher – a silent command consisting of pointing at a child who was talking or otherwise disrupting the class, and then pointing at the door.

This school had three rules: You had to be respectful to yourself and others, you couldn't damage school property, and you had to obey the go signal quietly and immediately.

When a student was given the go signal, they had to quietly walk out of the room into the hall and not return until they felt ready to work without disturbing others. Most of them merely did a quick turnaround in the hall and returned to their seats. If they thought it would take longer, they could go to a study hall until they were ready. If your school doesn't have a study hall, you could designate a small area of your classroom. If the child had received numerous go signals and the teacher could see that he was still disruptive, she would give him a "stop signal" by holding her hand out with the palm up. The student then had to stay out for the remainder of the period.

This strategy places the onus of responsibility on the child to determine whether they are ready or not to be in the classroom, and allows the teacher to maintain order without breaking the flow of work or give the child undue attention. It avoids power struggles because there are no angry words or sarcastic tone of voice used. It also prevents disruptive dialogues about what has taken place.

The two most important aspects of the go and stop signals are that they be given silently and that they are obeyed immediately. If a child disagrees with either signal, there should be an understanding that he can discuss it after class.

By observing this class, we could see that the respectful, non-confrontational approach of this technique was very well received by the children. It seemed to be taken more as a gentle reminder than a rebuke. This is particularly useful for undue attention seekers because they don't get a payoff. Teachers who tend to lecture or use too many words often unwittingly provide a great deal of attention when handling classroom disruptions. It's also effective for those seeking power because there is no opportunity to engage in a power struggle or an argument, plus it gives them control over when they come back.

# Goal Two:
# The mistaken goal of power

Every teacher recognizes the term "power struggle" and has experienced the frustration of battling with a defiant child who just won't give in. Ironically, these are strong-willed children who don't believe they are strong. They feel weaker than others, more inadequate and consequently resent control more. Children who have the mistaken goal of power seek significance by winning or not giving in, and they can only win when you lose or give in to their demands. They love to be the boss and feel that they only count when they are in control. This could include outsmarting the teacher with logic, stubbornly refusing to cooperate, open defiance, and even covert rebellion (they say yes but still don't cooperate).

*Kathryn, 15, is a grade 10 student who openly lets teachers know how she feels. Any homework assignment is met with complaints. She says the other teachers have already assigned homework and there is no way she can complete the work by tomorrow. Or, she complains that the homework is too difficult, or too easy, and a waste of time. She makes excuses why she couldn't hand in the work, which could range from family problems to personal respon-sibilities that didn't allow her time to complete the work. When told to come in after school and complete the work, she doesn't show up. Either she forgot or she had another appointment. After putting up with her defiance, her teacher now sends her out of class when she starts the complaints. She then complains to her parents that she doesn't know what the homework is. The parents are con-tinually calling the school accusing the teachers of picking on Kathryn. Guidance personnel have been brought in to help deal with her, but find her uncooperative and non-communicative.*

*Not doing her homework is only one aspect of her problem (power) behavior.*

As a teacher, the normal reaction would be to feel that your authority in the class is being challenged. Your first tactic will often be to try and overpower the child. Unfortunately, the more you try to win the power struggle, the more intense the battle becomes. A power struggle always produces a no-win situation. If the child wins, they feel so good to have won that they can become "drunk" with power and initiate more and more struggles to confirm their status. If you win the struggle, the child feels diminished by the loss. This creates an even stronger urge to fight you and may even stimulate them to revengeful behavior.

Once again, the only real answer is to sidestep the power struggle, stay out of conflict with the child, and find ways they can use their strengths to make contributions to the group.

As with all four goals, the child has to understand that they can have true significance through positive contributions.

## Behaviors that say "I want my own way":

- tantrums
- arguing
- tardiness
- refusing to work
- breaking rules
- not doing homework
- swearing

## Diagnosing the mistaken goal of power

1. How do you feel when the child misbehaves?
2. You will feel angry and worried that your authority is being threatened.
3. What are you thinking during the misbehavior? You might be thinking, "I can't let them get away with this. They have to…they must…do what I say." You  might even be wondering, "Who's the boss here? You, or me?" What does the child do when you intervene during the misbehavior? A "power child" will respond with resistance – they will deny, argue and/or be defiant. Even if they say, "OK, I'll stop," the behavior will continue in some way.

## Strategies for dealing with power struggles

The main strategy is to avoid being drawn into the power struggle in the first place. As we have already mentioned, this is a no-win situation for both you and the student. Instead of trying to tell the child what they must do, learn to be firm by telling them what you will do. Here are some examples of how to handle some common situations with firmness instead of domineering control techniques:

*Control Technique:* Demanding they be on time for class.
Using threats and angry words.
*Firmness:* You calmly start on time yourself no matter who is there.

*Control Technique:* Demand that everyone stop talking and making noise.
*Firmness:* Lower your own voice so that they can only hear you if they stop.

*Control Technique:* Punish all those who talk disrespectfully to you.
*Firmness:* Use a respectful tone with your students at all times. Lead by example.

It's very beneficial to give "power" students the recognition they deserve by pointing out their strengths and by admitting that there really is nothing anyone can do to force them to do things against their will. This signals that you are opting out of the struggle, which can disarm the child and stop a power struggle in its tracks.

Here are some helpful strategies for dealing with power struggles:

1. Don't give a "power child" direct orders or commands. Instead, let the situation dictate what needs to be done. For example: "It's time for…" rather than "Get to work right this minute."
2. Put power children into positions of responsibility. This

gives them power but in a way that benefits the group. Let them tutor younger students, organize committees, chair class meetings, or be responsible for specific jobs that need to be done in the classroom. Just make sure you give them guidance so they don't abuse these positions of power.

3. Avoid arguments at all costs. Arguments always end with a winner and a loser. Use the communications skills (like active listening, conflict resolution and problem solving) that are discussed in chapter 14 if you have a point of contention, and always talk through problems until you are both satisfied.

4. Give credit where credit is due. Acknowledge the areas these children excel at. Impress upon them that you don't want to argue, that you're not there to fight. Tell them you know they are strong, that they know their own mind, and that there is no way anyone can force them to do what they don't want to do.

## Other Strategies

✎ When you find yourself feeling backed into a corner, ask yourself: "Is it absolutely necessary that the child do this exactly when and the way I want it done?" Make sure you aren't becoming overly concerned with strict obedience, especially when the behavior is not breaking a school rule or affecting anyone else.

✎ Know yourself. Ask yourself if you are the kind of teacher who believes your classroom belongs to you. Do you like to make all the decisions yourself? Are you easily threatened or angered by defiance? If so, you should realize that you are more likely to have problems with this kind of child. Try to have fewer rules but be very consistent about the rules you do have so your students know the limits. Wherever possible, allow these children to work with you to solve the problems in a creative way. Remind yourself frequently not to take their defiance personally.

Understand that there is a degree of discouragement behind the behavior and that it will take a lot of encouragement to correct the problem.

Unfortunately, logical consequences and "power children" often don't mix. These children are so sensitive to control and manipulation that logical consequences are interpreted as punishment. Rely instead on natural consequences (chapter 7) and communication skills (chapter 14).

# Goal Three:
# The mistaken goal of revenge

Revenge often follows fast on the heels of power. When our attempts to control and dominate become intense and persistent enough, the child begins to feel that you do not like or "love" them, or perhaps even that they are unlovable, and that you are in fact trying to hurt them. They often feel rejected by the group and have long given up hope of winning the power struggle. They feel that the world is against them in a very "me against them" point of view. Revengeful children feel that a good offense is the best defense. They feel that there is an injustice being done to them, and that gives them permission to carry out their revenge without empathy for others. Instead, their thoughts and energies turn to ways of getting even.

The revengeful child's behavior can be vicious and violent, involving willful destruction of property, or more subtle violence, such as hurting people psychologically where they are vulnerable.

The goal of revenge indicates an extremely discouraged child whose goal is to hurt others. The real difficulty in working with this child is that his hurtful behavior ostracizes him from the group, justifying his feelings of revenge. The reaction of the group has therefore confirmed his belief that they are against him, creating a vicious circle that the teacher must break.

## Behaviors that hurt

✎ calling people names – "You're so fat" or "Loser!"
✎ destroying school property
✎ physical violence: hitting, hair pulling, biting, scratching, or kicking
✎ stealing
✎ immoral behavior
✎ self-destructive behaviors

## Diagnosing Revenge

1. What does the child do when you intervene? When the child is corrected he continues until he is successful in hurting the teacher or whoever else is in his sights.
2. How do you feel while the misbehavior is happening? You feel hurt, vulnerable, and disappointed.
3. What are you thinking during the behavior? You think, "How could he be so cruel and mean?" Or even, "I don't like this child."

## Strategies for the mistaken goal of revenge

The general strategy is to change the child's conviction that he is not liked or a part of the group. We have to convince him that he really is a part of the group, that he is likable and has a positive contribution to make just like everyone else. It's best to work with him to make rules so he sees how rules are made and that they are fair. Make sure there are no hints of favoritism. When he has done something wrong and hurtful, make sure there is no personal attack on him and that you make a distinction between the doer and the deed. "We like you, but not what you did."

1. Her goal is to hurt others, so make sure you don't provide the payoff she is seeking. If the child's revenge is aimed at the teacher, it's important that the teacher not be hurt by her actions. If she succeeds in hurting you she gets her pay-

off and therefore her significance.

2. Do not use punishments, criticism, or logical consequences.

3. Work with the group to help them become more accepting of the revengeful child. Use a sociometric test (see chapter 15) to see if there is anyone suitable who would be willing to "buddy up" with him for projects and other related work.

4. Surprise her by doing unexpected things that will make her feel happy or special – drop a note of appreciation on her desk right out of the blue (not as a reward, just as a surprise). Make sure you do this kind of thing for the other students as well.

5. Launch a campaign of extreme encouragement and positive affirmations.

6. Be friendly.

7. If you sense that the child has been hurt by something you have done, talk to her and apologize. Let her know you didn't mean to hurt her.

8. In the case of extreme revenge, seek counseling for the child.

## Goal Four: The mistaken goal of assumed inadequacy

This problem is really about the child's perception of himself. The child with this goal has come to the conclusion that there is no hope of being successful at the tasks of life. He believes that in one way or another he is not as capable or as competent as others. He has in essence given up and will not make an effort to face up to any of the challenges in his life. It is disheartening for parents and teachers to have to watch the passive, defeatist tendencies of this child. He does not want to be put to the test. His goal is, quite simply, to be left alone. He wants to avoid all pressure and situations where he might fail. From the outside he appears passive and withdrawn, often standing quietly at the side, always out of the action. This allows him to be easily ignored, but it also means he doesn't learn or progress that much.

This avoidance can occur on many different fronts, but it can also occur only in one area, such as athletics, or math, or social situations. This deep discouragement does not have anything to do with the child's real ability to overcome challenges, however. After all, some children with real disabilities manage to overcome them and function very well.

Of all the four goals, this is often the most misunderstood, because unlike the other goals, assumed inadequacy is not acted out by breaking rules or by doing something wrong and is therefore easily overlooked.

## Behaviors that say "I can't do it – leave me alone!"

- ✎ poor school performance
- ✎ withdrawal
- ✎ an unwillingness to try
- ✎ helplessness
- ✎ over-cautiousness

## Diagnosing assumed inadequacy

1. What does the child do when you intervene? The child refuses to try and continues with the withdrawn behavior.
2. How do you feel during the misbehavior? You develop a feeling of hopelessness and give up expecting anything from the child.
3. What are your thoughts during the misbehavior? You start to truly believe that there is something wrong with the child. You start to see them as incompetent and begin to think about things such as testing.

## Strategies for assumed inadequacy

If you have any serious doubts about the child's abilities, it's important to have them tested in order to rule out underlying physiological causes. However, you have to keep two things in mind: 1. A very discouraged child who has never put in any effort may score low on an intelligence test simply because their level of discouragement keeps them from trying. If a three-year old stops trying, by the time they are six they will score low no matter what their abilities are because they are behind. Therefore, you should be careful about interpreting test results. 2. The psychological state of the child can be the most important variable, even if the tests reveal that the child has some kind of learning or organic disability. After all, think of how someone like Helen Keller who managed to overcome huge physical challenges to become an extremely accomplished woman.

1. Never allow the child to hang back and withdraw. They want you to leave them alone so they won't have to be put to the test again and possibly fail. Don't let them achieve their goal. Don't give up on them.
2. Constantly bring them back to the group by saying things like, "Lets give it a try." "I believe in you." "I know you can do it." "I know you think you can't do this but I know you can."
3. Point out any improvements even if they are very small. Say things like, "Remember where you were? Look where you are now."
4. Set small, easily achieved goals for the child.
5. Most important of all is to focus on the efforts they make and not on the end result.

## Disclosing the goal

Parents are never advised to disclose the goal of the misbehavior to their children, mainly because they have too close a relationship. The child may feel that the parent is trying to psychoanalyze or manipulate them. But as a teacher who has the role of an educator, your relationship with the child is not as close and therefore more objective, allowing you to explore psychological goals together.

The best place to do this is in the class meeting, where you can use the entire group to make helpful suggestions and provide ongoing help. Ask the student if this is okay with her. If she says no, (children with a power goal are the least likely to go along with this) do it one-on-one.

Start with Goal One (Attention Seeking) and work your way down the list of four (sometimes there is more than one goal. Ask the child if she knows why she is misbehaving. "Why do you think you are talking out in class?"). Since the goal is unconscious, she will usually say she doesn't know. Ask her if she minds if you try and guess why she is doing it. Usually the child will agree. Always begin the question with "Could it be..." Start with your best guess. "Could it be that you like to have people pay attention to you?" If she says no and there is no recognition reflex (see page 60), keep going by asking questions about the other three goals.

When you get a positive response – either a verbal agreement or a nonverbal recognition reflex, you know you have succeeded in bringing the child's unconscious goal into their conscious mind. The cat is out of the bag. You now have a specific direction to continue the conversation in and can therefore work on an effective solution.

Ask the child what suggestions he has that would help him overcome the problem. If he has no ideas, turn to the class for suggestions. Ask questions like: "What do you think we could do to help Avery stop wanting so much attention?" (Note: the teacher has to explain that if the class keeps responding to

Avery's antics, he is getting the payoff he wants and the problem will continue. In order to help him, we can't give him attention when he is fooling around.) Using open-ended questions and problem-solving techniques (see chapter 13), you will come up with helpful solutions, such as "We won't laugh at him when he fools around, but we can recognize him when he does things that are good for the class." Then ask Avery: "If the class did that, do you think it might help you?"

Here are some questions that will help you disclose each of the four goals:

## Undue attention seeking

✎ "Could it be that you want to be noticed?"
✎ "Could it be that you want to be the centre of attention?"

## Power

✎ "Could it be that you want to show that you are the boss?"
✎ "Could it be that you don't want to be bossed around and controlled?"
✎ "Could it be that you don't like to take orders?"
✎ (For older kids) "Could it be that you don't like to feel manipulated?"

## Revenge

✎ "Could it be that you want to hurt other people because they hurt you?"
✎ "Could it be that you want to get even with people?"
✎ "Could it be that you want to get revenge?"

## Assumed Inadequacy

✎ "Could it be that you want people to give up on you because you feel there is no hope?"
✎ "Could it be that you want people to leave you alone?"

## THE RECOGNITION REFLEX

The recognition reflex is a spontaneous, uncontrollable response to hearing out loud what your unconscious goal is. Up until the time it is spoken out loud, you are not aware of it in a conscious way. That's why there is always some kind of physical response, such as a smile, or raised eyebrows, or eyes lighting up signaling that you have hit the nail on the head.

If you get the recognition reflex but the child still verbally denies it, it may be because they don't want to give up the game. Point it out to them. "You are saying no but your eyes are saying that it's true."

A final thought on the four goals is that they can and should be taught like any other subject so that your students can begin to understand the real meaning of the behavior of both their peers and themselves. This will also provide a reference point for discussions in the class meeting. One high school teacher created a chart in his class that listed the four goals of misbehavior. Whenever they discussed problems – such as students being late or skipping school – they referred to the chart to try and determine the purpose.

# CHAPTER 6

# What's wrong with punishment and rewards?

## Punishment

Punishment can only be given by a person in a superior position. Social equals cannot punish each other. Today, people living in a democratic society challenge the right of people in an authority position to punish those in a lesser position. Everyone feels they have rights, and punishment does not respect these rights.

In the autocratic teaching model of the past, punishment and rewards were the accepted means of motivating children. Everything from yelling, humiliation, and making children stand in the corner to actual hitting of the hands with a leather strap was practiced. It was the teacher's responsibility to make a child comply with the rules. And, in a limited way, this model worked, because when the punishment is severe enough, you can make the child do or stop doing just about anything. But at what price and for how long? The real focus of anyone attempting to instill discipline in a classroom should be to create intrinsic motivation, and to promote problem-solving skills and social interest. Punishment accomplishes absolutely none of this, but merely short-term behavioral change accompanied by many other negative outcomes.

Fortunately, today's teachers are recognizing that punishment does not seem to do the trick, and that it's also not in line with today's philosophical ideals. First of all, corporal punishment is frowned upon in our society. Schools and other authority figures don't rely on it any more. This is partly due to changing social values, but also because spanking has been shown to not only be ineffective but can also lead to psychological problems such as anti-social behavior, anxiety and substance abuse later in life. Children themselves have a sense that punishment is unfair in our democratic society. Even when punishment does seem to change behavior for the moment, the child is usually complying out of fear. In other words, there is a price to pay for punishing children. Their fear can bring on anger, resentment, and rebellion, which can harm the teacher-child relationship and have a lifelong negative effect.

## The obedience dilemma

It's important for children to listen to us and follow directions, but we have learned from past experiences that unquestioning obedience is not a desirable trait.

A few decades ago a famous psychology experiment was conducted in which an authority figure, dressed appropriately in a white lab coat, told students being tested to ask questions of another student wired up to a device that supposedly delivered electric shocks. They were instructed to zap the other student whenever they gave a wrong answer. The voltage was increased every time, until the other student would scream with pain and plead to not be shocked again. "Keep going," the lab-coated scientist would urge, and almost every student obeyed. The result was a chilling indictment of blind obedience.

We punish to get strict obedience, but this is not really a healthy, desirable response. Perhaps the most important reason to question the use of punishment is the interpretation the child makes about himself and others. This interpretation will affect all aspects of his life because children, especially those below the age of seven, are constantly trying to draw conclusions about who they are and what their relationship is with other people.

One strong danger of using punishment to control a child's behavior is that children may think of other people as being:

✎ mean or cruel
✎ unfair or unjust
✎ "against me"
✎ powerful, domineering, controlling
✎ not to be trusted

Equally possible is that they will begin to view themselves as:

✎ weak
✎ a victim
✎ a bad person

One last danger is that those that are taught to follow blindly may follow other, more anti-social groups in order to be accepted.

As you can see, punishment can shape how the child views himself in a negative way. The "good" kids, those who can usually stay out of trouble, don't get a lot of punishment. Ironically, they are the ones best able to deal with punishment because they are the ones with the highest self-esteem. Even when they do mess up, their attitude is apt to be something like: "I made a mistake, but I'm still okay. I'll just try not to do it again." Their self-esteem remains intact, but the kids with low self-esteem are the ones who get punished the most and are the most likely to jump to the conclusion that there is therefore something wrong with them and/or others.

The truth is, not every child will take punishment the same way. They rarely think that punishment is fair, and often they are right. A child forgets to bring his homework in so he has to stay in at recess and clean the blackboards. She doesn't see the connection and she's right – there isn't one.

Children are usually more tenacious and creative than adults. They also don't feel as bound by social restraints as we do – most adults wouldn't break something when they are angry, for example, or hit someone to get revenge. The result is that teachers often run out of ideas and energy. They don't know what to do when the punishments don't work. Often, these punishments go on day after day. You have to ask yourself: If I believe punishment works, why do I have to keep doing it? Why am I spending half my class time being a cop? The truth is, when we use power techniques in child rearing or in teaching, it often brings about rebellion without instilling cooperation. Another problem is that punishments tend to escalate. You come up with a punishment and if it doesn't work, the tendency is to give another, harder punishment, and so on. This can create rebellion, anger and even revengeful behavior in a child who feels they have been wronged.

Perhaps the most puzzling aspect of punishment is that we believe people must suffer in order to learn a lesson. You really have to wonder where this came from. Yet even though we know it doesn't work (the high recidivist rate of prisons is one tip-off), our entire judicial system is based upon it.

In order for someone to undergo a positive change, such as remembering to bring homework back to class, for example, they have to want to start being responsible. They have to feel motivated, which is unlikely if they are seething in anger because they feel the punishment was unjust.

Besides, no matter how much you might want to pretend otherwise, punishments are often handed out in anger. The child does the wrong thing for the umpteenth time and that can be annoying, so you want to strike out and give them something to think about. If we are totally honest, we have to admit that it's not always done to help the child learn. Sometimes it's done to strike back at someone who you think (often rightly) is trying to defeat you. You are then acting out of your own feelings of inadequacy and frustration because you can't get your students to do what you want them to do.

To sum up, punishment is only good for temporary, not fundamental change. It doesn't work in the long run because the desired behavior doesn't come from within the child, but is imposed externally. The child doesn't change the behavior because she wants to, but only to please an authority figure or to avoid unpleasantness.

## Rewards

Stickers, gold stars, candy, small gifts like books and pencil erasers, and even high grades and special privileges if you're good – rewards in the classroom take all kinds of forms.

This is another tool of the autocratic approach: giving a treat or a special privilege for doing the right thing. It's very popular right now because a lot of teachers see it as a tangible reinforcement for good behavior and good work. It's also seen as being fair and equitable. But in the long run, rewards don't work any better than punishment, and in fact teaches the wrong values because it is a manipulative tool.

When good behavior is followed up with treats and privileges, children eventually begin to think "I've got something coming to me if I do the right thing." This creates an expectation and they get angry when it's not fulfilled. In contrast to the goals of social interest, which are to lead the child toward feelings of empathy towards others and being helpful to the group, rewards bring the focus back to "what's in it for me?" When rewards are given (as they usually are) to a select few, this results in a jostling for position to receive the handouts, which heightens competition and encourages self interest instead of social interest.

In one instance we know of, a teacher promised highly prized sporting tickets to the four best-behaved students in his class. This "behavioral beauty contest" created such feelings of animosity towards the teacher and jealousy towards the winners that the class was in upheaval for days. Here are some remarks we heard from the losers: "That was unfair." "What a stupid contest." "So and so didn't even deserve it." At no time did any of the students who lost express a desire to improve their behavior so they could win next time. Competition was heightened and a division was made between the "good kids" who will always win the rewards, and the "bad kids" who are having difficulties and therefore usually don't win.

At the root of the concept of rewards is a long-held prejudice towards children. There is a mistaken belief that children don't want to do the right thing naturally, so we have to employ either a carrot or a stick. But we believe that children have a deeply rooted desire to do the right thing and enjoy the benefits of cooperative behavior the same way adults do. You have only to see the delight on the face of a child when they begin to learn how to read to understand this. That is their real reward – the accomplishments and improvements they make and the joy of being fully absorbed in an activity. Rewards take the focus away from these efforts and accomplishments and put it back on the carrot, ultimately becoming a seductive distraction from the natural joys of learning and cooperating.

This was graphically illustrated in a recent television program. In trying to determine whether or not rewards worked, two young boys were given pencils and told to trace out a maze. The first boy was told he would be given money for participating, the second boy was offered no such reward. After a short period (before the puzzle was completed), the boys were told to stop. The first boy stopped immediately and held out his hand for his money. The second boy, however, kept on tracing the maze, completely absorbed in his task. One did it for someone else, the other for himself.

Rewards undermine the natural desire to cooperate, and substitute a "what's in it for me?" attitude. In addition, through the manipulation that is inherent in the giving of rewards, a child may feel controlled and overpowered.

Rewards can also have a discouraging effect on academic achievement.

*Lucy was in grade two and doing just fine on her spelling tests, receiving happy face stickers as rewards for her work. She came to anticipate and expect these little pats on the back. But eventually the tests became more difficult and Lucy's marks got worse. The happy face stickers stopped appearing. Lucy didn't like that. She started checking those around her and would get particularly upset if she was the only one who wasn't getting stickers. She began to not want to do spelling. She started to give up. That meant the stickers still didn't come. She covered up her discomfort by saying things like: "Spelling is stupid. It's not important anyway. I hate spelling!" This was the beginning of Lucy's lack of effort with this subject.*

The idea that rewards don't have any place in a democratic classroom is sometimes a hard one to grasp, but in a relationship of social equals, rewards are inappropriate. It's true that rewards are motivating for students who are excelling, which is why a lot of teachers use them, however, for those who aren't on the receiving end, rewards can result in resistance, rebelliousness and anger, just as they do with punishment. We need to move on to a new child-rearing technique – one that develops cooperative behavior. In place of reward and punishment, encouragement, as well as natural and logical consequences, should be used. In this approach, the child is treated as a partner and a social equal.

# CHAPTER 7

# Consequences – taking responsibility for your choices

## Natural consequences

There are two kinds of consequences: natural and logical. Simply put, a consequence is the result of an action. Every choice we make, every action we take, has a consequence. A natural consequence is a result that nature imposes ("nature" is, after all, the root of the word "natural"). Life provides us with countless learning opportunities like this. If a bike is left out in the rain, it will become rusty and unusable. If we don't eat because mom packed tuna fish again, we will be hungry. If we don't wear a warm jacket in December, we are cold. If we don't put a rock on our papers, they will blow away. If our hand-held computer game is left on, the batteries will run out. These are forces of nature and you can't argue with them. They exist and you have to learn how to live within their limits. These kinds of cause-and-effect experiences teach our children why some choices are better than others without our having to impose a correction. This minimizes teacher-student conflict –

after all, it's hard to blame the teacher when your baseball glove got ruined because you left it out in the rain. With natural consequences, the teacher doesn't interfere but lets nature take its course.

Obviously, there is a common sense aspect to using natural consequences. And yet, there is a resistance to it. This resistance comes from the fact that teachers and parents are primed to nurture and watch out for the children under their care. This makes it difficult for them to stand back and do nothing – letting nature take its course. But natural consequences are such a powerful learning process that it is important to guard against becoming overprotective or pampering. Your job is to find the common sense midpoint between being overprotective and being too lax. Think of yourself as a filter, whose purpose is to let children learn the necessary life lessons without undergoing serious harm.

As long as they're not dangerous, mistakes are good things. By following age-appropriate guidelines, children can be made responsible for their own actions. By allowing children to see the results of their choices, in effect, to reap what they sow, consequences turn common mistakes and misbehaviors into learning opportunities. We know one teacher who has a chart at the front of her class labeled "LO" for "Learning Opportunities." She told her students that no one in her class makes mistakes, instead they are afforded learning opportunities. Whenever they are unhappy with an outcome, she would ask them to write it on the chart, including what they learned and what they could do differently next time. This is a great example of putting a positive spin on what is traditionally a negative event. The teacher's job is to provide advice, guidance and information about the laws of nature. It is up to the child whether or not he follows through with the advice.

Consequences are also great at keeping you from getting caught between the child and the learning experience. They do this by putting the emphasis on the child's choice and helping him take responsibility for that choice, rather than the teacher trying to make him do the right thing. This helps children see consequences as being more fair.

Natural consequences are a great way to learn but they unfortunately can't be used when the child's choices are unsafe or unethical (doing handstands on top of the monkey bars, for example). For these instances, you must intervene and prevent nature from taking its course and use logical consequences instead.

# Logical consequences

A logical consequence is an unpleasant or inconvenient experience that results directly from the child's actions. Unlike natural consequences, however, these logical outcomes are arranged by the teacher and/or the class. Right now you are probably gleefully rubbing your hands together in anticipation of handing out some nice, juicy consequences to your "favorite" students. If that is your intent, you have unfortunately missed the point. It's not about making students pay for what they have done wrong, but about their learning something from their actions. In order for it to work, there has to be a logical thread between the child's behavior and the outcome you and the class have arranged (which punishments don't have).

Like natural consequences, logical consequences provide situations that teach children about the choices they make. What, for example, is the logical consequence of not doing your homework? It might be that you have to complete it at another time, such as at recess or lunch hour. What if one student, or even the whole class, is making noise and not listening? The teacher can stop teaching until the class quiets down and begins to listen. The consequence here, simple as it may be, is that the class cannot be taught unless it pays attention. The beauty of this approach is that most children readily see the connection between the behavior and the consequence. Punishment, on the other hand, is almost always seen as being an arbitrary, often unfair decision made by the "nasty old teacher."

By assuring there is a connection between the behavior and the outcome, consequences also help children have a more realistic understanding of life's problems. For instance, there are many ways to solve a problem or cope with a stressful situation. When a consequence occurs it forces us to look for an alternative course of action.

*Your students have agreed that if the class got its own gerbil, they would be in charge of feeding it. But there has been some difficulty getting the students to feed the gerbil every day as they had promised. You decide to take the gerbil and give it temporarily to another class. When the children notice the gerbil has been removed, you can say: "I had to place the gerbil where I could count on the fact that she would be fed every day." At this point the children will probably promise to feed the gerbil faithfully because they want her back. Tell them you would like to have the gerbil back as well, but you will have to talk about it at a class meeting. Here is where the creativity starts. The unhappiness the logical consequence produced spurs the children on to find ways of solving the problem together. In the class meeting, the focus is on how to help each other remember to feed the gerbil. They will probably come up with things like feeding schedules, reminders, a job monitor, or a chart that can be ticked off every time the gerbil is fed. This is the creative process at work.*

In addition to solving problems, consequences are great for learning simple, practical life skills, such as how to use a screwdriver or clean up a mess.

*In a kindergarten class of five-year-olds, one of them drops some labels down a heating vent for fun. As a logical consequence, he uses a screwdriver to take the screws out of the vent and retrieve the labels. In the process of learning why we don't put labels down the vent, he also learned how to use a screwdriver.*

We have to use our own creativity when thinking of appropriate consequences for the misbehaviors children present. If we are used to using punishments (which are arbitrary), it's sometimes difficult to make the transition to using consequences, which have to actually make sense. Some teachers express difficulty in knowing where to begin. One trick is to always try and create a situation that mimics real life as closely as possible. Try and imagine what would happen if you didn't interfere. Here are some examples to lead you in the right direction. As you will see, there are often many different appropriate consequences for each problem.

### Misbehavior
A student is late for class.

### Outcome if teacher doesn't intervene
✎ Material is missed
✎ The student disturbs the class when she comes in late

### Possible logical consequence
✎ Student must get missed material from someone else and stay late to copy it.
✎ Student is asked to sit at the back of the classroom, until there is a break, so she doesn't interfere with the concentration of others.
✎ Student misses out on the material covered and is therefore not prepared for tests.

### Misbehavior
Throwing litter from lunches onto the playground.

### Outcome if teacher doesn't intervene
✎ The playground looks unattractive.
✎ The spoiled food could attract insects and vermin.
✎ School morale suffers.

### Possible logical consequence
✎ Students have to pick up the litter, either on their own time or at recess.
✎ Students have to eat their lunch in the classroom until they learn to clean up after themselves.

✎ Clean-up monitors are assigned to make sure the playground is kept clean.

✎ Litterless lunches are inaugurated.

Thinking about what would happen if you didn't intervene is a good way to start trying to come up with consequences of your own. Deciding what a good consequence would be gets easier with practice.

When using consequences with a particular student, it is important to understand the goals of the child's misbehavior (See The Four Goals of Uncooperative Behavior, Chapter 5). If the child is seeking undue attention, logical consequences work well. On the other hand, (as we have pointed out in the previous chapter) children seeking power may view a logical consequence as punishment, or as just another aspect of the control the teacher is trying to exert over them.

If you are going to use a consequence and you know the goal of the misbehavior is power, be sure to include the child in the discussion of what is to be done, always offering them choices.

## The difference between consequences and punishment

✎ Consequences are solution-oriented. Punishments are hurtful.

✎ Consequences are aimed at teaching life skills. Punishments focus on past mistakes.

✎ Consequences focus on the deed. Punishments focus on the doer.

✎ Consequences are seen as coming from the child's actions. Punishments are seen as coming from the teacher's will.

✎ Consequences are stated in a calm, respectful tone of voice. Punishments are issued with a sharp tongue.

✎ Consequences don't disturb the relationship between student and teacher. Punishments often interfere with the relationship.

✎ Consequences maintain the child's self-esteem. Punishments hurt the child's self-esteem.

✎ Consequences are viewed as being fair. Punishments are seen as being unfair and arbitrary.

✎ Consequences teach the rules of social living. Punishments teach children to avoid getting caught.

## Tips for consequences

✎ The easiest way to turn a consequence into a punishment is by adding an admonishment at the end, such as: "I hope you've learned your lesson now." This not only makes the child feel worse about what they have done, it quickly undoes the lesson the child has learned by adding a critical remark. Hold back when tempted to add a little moral lesson of your own to the consequence.

✎ Ask yourself, how would I feel in their shoes? Does the consequence seem fair, logical, and equal to the problem?

✎ Always build a second chance into the consequence. Let the child determine when they are ready to try again (which helps them develop responsibility).

✎ For common, recurring problems, consequences can be determined in advance at the class meeting by the whole group. This not only hones their problem-solving skills, but detaches the teacher even more from the consequence.

✎ Watch your tone of voice and body language. If you are angry, wait until you calm down to devise and impose a consequence.

There is a lot of confusion around what is and what isn't a consequence. You will know that something is a consequence when:

✎ The child has been given a choice.

✎ A second chance for the child has been built into the consequence ("You are disturbing the class so you have to work on your own. You can come back when you are ready").

✎ It is focused on the future, and not the past. This usually involves teaching the kids to take positive action in order to correct their mistakes. This may include, for example, cleaning up a mess they have made, apologizing for insulting someone, or using their own money to replace something they have broken.

## Logical Consequences are only used when:

✎ An agreed-upon rule has been established.
✎ The consequences are helpful, and not hurtful.

If there are no consequences that readily present themselves to you, there probably isn't one and you should proceed directly to problem solving (chapter 13) in order to deal with the misbehavior. For example, let's say two students exchange competitive putdowns (this can often happen under the guise of being funny but it is hurtful none the less) on the playground. One of them, more sensitive to the nuances of criticism and rejection, ends up crying in the washroom. You can't think of a consequence that will form any kind of a learning situation. You're right, there really aren't any. There are two possible ways to go in this instance: One is to ask the two students if they would mind talking about it at a class meeting. If they say no, you may have to do some two-person problem solving with the students alone.

## Following through

Firmness and following through are also important. Let the students know what you are willing to do and not do. By not telling them what they have to do, you are offering them a choice.

On a personal note, as a young teacher, I used to try to get my young students in on time from lunch and recess by yelling at them and using threats. In desperation, I even set up a reward system for the early birds. I also wasted a lot of time cajoling them into getting seated and settling down. It wasn't until I started my lesson right on time regardless of who was present, that the children started to respect and see the importance of being on time. The consequences of being late were:

- ✎ The students who were ready to begin were distracted and annoyed by the late comers – and they let them know. The consequence was having their peers annoyed with them.
- ✎ They missed important information that was being presented.
- ✎ They didn't like the stigma of the latecomer.

To teach them the social importance of being on time (because being late disturbs others), the class could all agree that the children who came in late should not be allowed to interrupt the lesson. They would therefore have to wait until there was a break in the activity before they could take their place in the group. This consequence will also encourage parents to bring their children to school on time.

Sometimes a logical consequence has to happen quickly and spontaneously. Fighting is one example. Another is when a student is causing damage to school property like breaking chalk, disfiguring a desk with a marker, or throwing a ball near the windows. In these cases, you would have to intervene immediately. You would take away the chalk, the marker, or the ball, to be returned when the student lets you know they are ready to use them properly. Of course repairing or replacing damaged school property should be part of school policy.

If you are having an ongoing problem, you sometimes have to sit down at a neutral time and work it out with the child. For example, a student is being repeatedly rude and disrespectful to you. Through discussion (discover the child's goal and feelings using active listening and problem solving techniques), you must also explain that you are not willing to be in the room with someone who is treating you that way. The next time it happens, the child will have to leave the room until he is ready to behave respectfully (this shows the teacher has respect for himself).

From now on the child knows what to expect from this kind of misbehavior. To reinforce this, it is important to be both consistent and act quickly so that the misbehavior does not go on for a long time.

## Punishment – Consequences Chart

Sometimes teachers or others in positions of authority will think they are using consequences but they are really punishing. Why the confusion? For one thing, it's not "politically correct" to be seen punishing these days, so people call it "consequences." Nice try, but if you give out a detention for talking in class, have students write lines for not doing homework, or some other consequence that has no connection with the behavior, that's punishment. There are a lot of subtle and not so subtle differences between consequences and punishment. Here are some common behaviors, along with possible consequences, as well as the more commonly used punishments.

*Behavior*
Bullying

*Natural consequences*
✎ The other kids won't play with you.

*Logical consequences*
✎ Separate the bully from the group and let them come back when they think they are ready. The follow-up would be to have some problem-solving sessions about bullying at the class meeting so everyone, even the child who was bullying, can talk about what the goal of the behavior is and what can be done about it.

*Punishments*
✎ Suspension from school (for a definite period of time)
✎ Having the parents called to the school for the purpose of punishing the student at home
✎ Detentions

✎ Yelling and lecturing

✎ Humiliation (in front of the child's peers)

## *Behavior*
Talking in class and disturbing others.

## *Logical consequences*
✎ Give the "Go" signal (see page 47). The child must leave the room until she can come back and not disturb others.

✎ Child must make up missed work on her own time.

✎ The teacher stops and waits for quiet.

## *Punishment*
✎ Writing lines

✎ Detentions

✎ Has to leave the room (ordered out angrily – "Get out!")

✎ Humiliation ("If Mr. Chatterbox would be quiet for a second, we could get on with our lesson.")

# CHAPTER 8

# Building rapport

B eing a teacher is a "people job." To be good at this job it's important to like people, to accept them for who they are, and to be interested in the complexity of human relationships. It's also important to be genuine and comfortable with yourself. Above all else, the teachers who actually like being around kids, who enjoy their company and the particular kind of energy that children have, will be the best at their craft. And it's important that you are good at this job, because if you do it right you can have a positive, lifelong impact on a developing child.

Some people begin teaching because of their love for, and knowledge of, a particular subject that they want to share with others. This is commendable, but if that's your only reason, you should aim for the university level because it won't be enough for the lower grades. With younger kids, you shouldn't confuse the love of a subject with the love of people. With younger kids, your real job is not just to impart information, but to instill the love of learning. To motivate and ignite their passion for understanding and exploration. This does not necessarily follow from the mastery of a subject alone.

We once had a teacher in high school who had actually written the math text that the course was based on. He couldn't have known the subject better but he couldn't have taught it worse. Compounding the situation was that if you went to him for help, you went away feeling stupid for not getting it. His impatience showed as he talked down to the students who were struggling, leaving them feeling they were not up to par. His mastery of the subject overshadowed his compassion for the students trying to learn it.

You can spot the teachers who really care about their students. Here are some ideas on how you can show that you care:

✎ We know of one teacher who phones new students before their first day at school, or writes them a letter in the summer just to introduce himself, to tell them how much they are going to enjoy their year and how much he is looking forward to it. This is just one of the ways he has of saying, "I'm interested in you as a person."

✎ We know of another teacher who set up a chessboard in the back of her class so her students could use it when they were finished their work. It was something the teacher found interesting and thought maybe her students would as well. As it turned out, they did. In fact chess became a big thing in her class and even spilled over to the rest of the school, with chess tournaments being staged. In this way, the teacher came up with an idea that built on common interest to get everyone working together on something.

The point is that the key to excellent teaching is in creating a good relationship with each child. To do that you have to genuinely care about them because that is an integral part of encouragement and motivation. But in doing that, in your commendable attempt to create a bond between yourself and your students, be careful not to try and be something you are not. In order to gain the respect and trust of children, you have to first of all be yourself. You can't wear a mask in the classroom. Your students watch you every day. They know your every mood and mannerism and even your wardrobe. You can't fool them so don't even try. If you are fun-loving, let it show in class. If you are quiet and reserved by nature, be that way.

The flip side of this coin is to accept your students as they are. If you do nothing else, do that, because one of the best ways to get close to your students is to take the nonjudgmental route. The worst thing you can do is look upon them as flawed works in progress who must be bent into a new shape by you in order to be considered alright.

Share your interests with them (like the teacher with the passion for chess). Tell them about your family, your hobbies, your likes and dislikes – all the things that make you human. Mind you this can be taken too far. Some teachers will talk about themselves until the cows come home, which can be off-putting ("He talks about his kids all the time!").

You should also hone your sense of humor. Being humorous tends to lessen the possibility for discouragement (unless someone is the butt of the joke), and a light, humorous approach can bring about an optimism regarding problems.

## Can teachers and students really be friends?

One test of how much the teacher-child relationship has changed is that we can even ask this question. As we have already pointed out, in the old days the teacher ruled through fear – fear of punishment, failing grades, humiliation, and intimidation. Being friends was not considered desirable or appropriate. But now things have changed, so much so that many teachers are unsure of what their relationship is with students.

Today's teacher-student relationship is a very unique one. Essentially, the teacher's job is still to help the child learn the curriculum and achieve a certain maturity, while the student's job is to cooperate with this and apply themselves to learning. Of course as the class leader, you still have tremendous influence, it's just that you now operate in a democratic atmosphere. The new relationship is based on social equality, which means it is based on mutual respect and choice even though you are not equal in knowledge or experience. You can never be true friends (in the social sense of the word) with your students because the responsibility and roles of both parties are set, whereas with friends it is not. You never reveal deeply personal problems to your students ("I'm having a lot of trouble with my spouse"). You grade your students, but you never grade your friends. You are responsible for your students but not your friends. But you can and should cultivate a relationship with your students based on friendliness and caring. Just be sure you spread it around equally. Playing favorites (like having a "teacher's pet") is very destructive. Strive for a truly democratic classroom.

## Teacher's pet

In our experience, children constantly complain about the "teacher's pet" problem. It's a lot like children in a family who see one sibling as the favorite. Of course, there will always be students in your classroom who you click with better than the rest. One teacher will like exuberant children, while another will prefer the calm, quiet type. Some enjoy like-minded students who are into sports, while others prize reading and intellectual capability. It's human nature, but you should be aware of the fact that you might unconsciously favor children of a particular sex, ethnic background, attractiveness, or popularity.

Ways of showing favoritism:

- giving someone more attention than others
- holding them up as an example
- picking them for coveted chores or responsibilities
- changes in demeanor and expression when talking to a particular student are also subtle indicators of favoritism

When the students come to the realization that there is some favoritism taking place, resentment and anger are not far behind. This is bad for class morale and bad for the "pet's" relationships with the others.

Following democratic ideals, as well as removing rewards and punishments, will go a long way towards minimizing this problem.

# Dealing with personalities

In rare situations a child's personality doesn't mix with the teacher's. Both parties can find it impossible to create a good working relationship. This can happen, for example, when an overcritical teacher has an overly sensitive student, or a very controlling teacher is thrown together with a rebellious student. As with some marriages, sometimes the only answer to the situation is a divorce, and the child should be moved to another class. This is a last resort and should only be used when the child's emotional and academic wellbeing is threatened, and when all other avenues of problem solving have been exhausted.

Nine ways to build rapport

1. Have true and genuine respect for your students. This means things like yelling, belittling and bossing around are not in your repertoire. Instead, involve children in decision making, be respectful to them, and use good listening and communication techniques.

2. Accept all students as they are. This involves not trying to change them into who you think they should be. It also means trying to find the positive in all of them (everyone has it).

3. Determine their goals (their motivation). When a person feels understood, it immediately creates rapport. This is your chance to help students learn more about themselves in a nonjudgmental and supportive way.

4. Do lots of little things that let your students know you are interested in them. Remember their birthdays. Ask how they did at a big sporting event, or mention last night's NHL game if you know they're interested in hockey. It's a lot like a family, it can be the little things, the small gestures and remembrances, that mean so much.

5. Take an interest in their personal lives. If their family has a new baby or is involved in a special activity, mention it. Talk about their pets or special interests. One teacher we know got up early and attended a weekend soccer game several of

his students were playing in.

6. Be a real human being. Be relaxed in the classroom. Let your own personality shine through by letting your own interests be known. A good way to do this is to schedule a 10- or 20-minute news period that lets your students – and you – talk about something interesting that happened in your lives.

7. Have a sense of humor. This is more than just cracking jokes. It means laughing at someone else's jokes and finding the humor in all kinds of situations. Here's an example: instead of droning on with "now take out your math book and turn to page 43," use a little pizzazz, "And now, the moment you have all been waiting for – take out your math books and turn to (dramatic pause) PAGE 43!" The humor, however, should never be at the expense of someone else.

8. Set aside time for fun, for spontaneous things. All work and no play makes for a dull day. Bring in a radio, and right out of the blue, announce that if anyone can guess what song is playing on the (popular) radio station, the whole class will have a pizza party at the end of the year.

9. Make time for your students. Time is the great precious commodity we all hoard like misers. It's a given that we're all overworked and overstressed these days, but it's essential to make time for your students. Making time for kids who need extra help after school for schoolwork or personal problems, is a sure way to create a bond with them. Let them know during a class meeting that you are there for them if there is something they don't want to bring up at the meeting itself.

## THE PROBLEMATIC TEACHER

Here are some less than helpful characteristics some teachers have. Recognize anyone?

▼ **The Critic** (The irresistible urge to find the flaws in everyone, and then tell them about it.)

▼ **The Dominator** ("This class is my turf. I own you all!")

▼ **The Wet Noodle** (Totally permissive – no guidelines or authority.)

▼ **Mr. Un-excitement** (Hates the job and finds the kids a snore. Just killing time until the pension kicks in.)

▼ **The Absent Minded Professor** (Drives the kids nuts by being unorganized, unfocused, and without any clear goals or sense of where he is going.)

▼ **Mr. Superior** (Condescending and haughty, this person doesn't so much teach as make pronouncements to the Great Unwashed.)

▼ **The Know It All** (Can't wait for the student to flub the answer so she can exhibit her superior knowledge.)

▼ **The Center of the Universe** (Just a little self-centered. Can spend days showing you his family album.)

▼ **The Teacher's Pet Picker** (Chooses one person or a small clique of students, pushing the rest out of the inner circle of the chosen few.)

# CHAPTER 9

# What to do the first day

I deally, the first day will alleviate the anxieties your students will probably be experiencing before starting a new school year. After all, some of them may have had bad experiences in former years, and don't know what to expect from you. Everything done the first day, therefore, should begin the process of helping them to feel comfortable, motivating them to learn and work hard, as well as uniting the group socially.

Your goal on the first day should be to accomplish four basic tasks:

1. To set class goals for the year.
2. To create social guidelines for how you are going to behave towards each other.
3. To begin to establish the democratic process.
4. To begin the process of getting to know each other.

## Setting class goals

You primary aim here is to spark interest in the subjects you are going to teach. Give them an overview of all the subjects – the big picture as well as the highlights – so that they can say to themselves: "Gee, by the end of the year I will have learned all about X."

Say things like: "We're going to be doing a lot of reading this year about the pioneers. We'll be putting on a play about them, and even create our own pioneer village."

Use enthusiasm. Show your own interest and excitement about the subjects you are going to teach. Let them know that they will have input into how these subjects are covered, that you would be interested in hearing their ideas of how to make the curriculum more interesting.

## The democratic process

The ideal forum for the expression of the above ideal of respect is the class meeting. Talk to your class about what the meeting is (see chapter 10) and how it will work. Stress to your students that the class meeting will be used to make decisions together, plan special events, and solve difficulties.

This will probably be the first exposure your students have to the idea of a class meeting, so show them what a typical agenda might look like. Talk about when you will have the meetings, and the different roles they will take in conducting them.

Get them excited about it. Point out how good they are going to get at helping each other solve problems, in leading meetings, and just generally expressing their feelings and listening to each other.

One of the most important things to do that first day is to have an actual class meeting. It's never too early to get them used to the idea that class meetings will be held regularly over the year, and that they will be the most important decision-making mechanism the class will have. Briefly show them how the chairperson operates, as well as everything else pertaining to the running of a meeting. Hold a short (half-hour) meeting the first day with a follow-up meeting the next day and every day the first week to keep the ball rolling and to firmly establish the meeting format in their minds. After that you can hold them once a week.

You might want to structure your first class meeting around the idea of creating social guidelines.

## Creating social guidelines

Just as important as what you will be learning is how the class will function together socially. Think of it as the "social curriculum". Stress that you can only achieve the first goal – to learn – if you are all happy in the class and getting along with each other. Explain that the freedom to learn involves limits and responsibilities. Use the analogy that if everyone didn't agree to line up to get on a bus, everyone would be pushing and shoving and it would be much harder to get on the bus. Respect and cooperation help groups function better and accomplish more in a more pleasant way. Have a discussion on the basic social guidelines you will use to govern the social interplay within the classroom, which will be based on mutual respect. Talk about ways you can all demonstrate respect for each other.

The teacher and the class should then work together to come up with a set of "rules of respect", such as:

- being on time
- speaking to each other in respectful ways
- listening to each other
- eliminating put downs
- taking care of the physical classroom
- respecting yourself

This list will be added to as a result of decisions made in class meetings and other discussions.

# Ice Breakers

Try out some "ice breakers" to help get the class feeling like a team, especially for the ones who might not know each other. Here are some fun exercises to help the kids in your class get to know each other.

## The Interview Game

*Purpose:*

1. Getting to know a new classmate
2. Learning to become a better listener
3. Becoming more relaxed around people
4. Learning how to look for positive qualities in others

*Instructions:*

1. Ask the kids to make name tags for themselves
2. Have everyone sit in a circle next to someone they don't know well
3. The teacher hands out a sheet with questions and spaces for the answers to be written in. The students ask each other questions and fill in the answers (10 minutes each)
4. Introduce your partner to the class by using the answers to the questions you asked (1-3 minutes), and adding one thing that you found out about them that you liked (i.e., they were funny, interesting, a good listener, etc.,)

*Questions:*

(Note: these questions can vary according to age, and of course you can make up your own.)

1. What is the thing you enjoy doing the most?
2. What is your favorite TV show?
3. What do you like most/least about school?
4. How many brothers and sisters do you have?
5. Who is your favorite singer or band?
6. What's your favorite subject?
7. What is the best quality you have that makes you a good friend?
8. What quality do you look for in friends?
9. What thing are you the best at?
10. If you could have one wish, what would it be, and why?
11. What would you like to be/do when you grow up?

If anyone gets through answering the questions before the time is up, they can find out more about their new friend.

*Processing the Exercise:*

Ask each student the following questions:

1. How did you feel when interviewing your partner?
2. How did you feel when talking about your partner?
3. How did you feel when your partner was talking about you?
4. Is there any information about yourself that you would like to add?

## The Name Game

*Purpose:*

1. To learn everyone's first name.
2. To learn what each person enjoys doing.
3. To learn how to express your feelings in a group.

*Instructions:*

Split into three groups, each forming their own circle. The first person in each group starts by saying: "My name is Rebecca." The person sitting to the right of her says: "Your name is Rebecca and my name is Maria." The next person says each of the other two: "Your name is Rebecca, your name is Maria and my name is Randy."

After everyone has had a chance to recite the names of everyone in their group, they go around the circle again and add an additional quality: "My name is Rebecca and I enjoy acting." The next person says: "Your name is Rebecca and you enjoy acting. My name is Maria and I enjoy helping my mom cook," and so on around the circle.

Other statements that can be added are:

✎ How the person is feeling at the moment
✎ Their chores at home
✎ Favorite subject in school

## What animal would you be?

*Instructions:*

Everyone has a turn to tell the class what animal they would like to be if they weren't human. They also give two reasons why. Then they tell what animal they wouldn't want to be, and why. Younger children could draw the animals they want and don't want to be.

After each child has given their answers, the teacher categorizes their responses, taking into account what each person has volunteered about why they chose a certain animal:

✎ powerful (elephant)
✎ beautiful (cat)
✎ graceful (jaguar)
✎ fun (monkey)
✎ wise (owl)
✎ freedom loving (bird)
✎ friendly (dog)
✎ peaceful (dove)
✎ brave (lion)
✎ smart (dolphin)

This can very easily evolve into a discussion of what each student personally values.

## The Hot Seat

*Instructions:*

One person volunteers to sit in a chair at the front of the room. The class may ask the person five personal questions (e.g., "tell us one thing that you are particularly proud of"). The person doesn't have to answer a question if they don't want to.

All of these personal-sharing and team-building exercises are great for creating feelings of equality and decreasing feelings of inadequacy. When children feel inferior, it's because they are comparing themselves to others. These exercises help children feel that others who appear to be superior have problems similar to theirs. That to be human is to have weaknesses and fears. It also helps those who feel superior to understand others and to be more tolerant and friendly. To reinforce this feeling of togetherness, tell them that, after you get to know each other better, "we can all create a seating arrangement together."

The first day should be interesting, positive and exciting. Each student should end their day looking forward in some way to coming back the next day, and they will if you have managed to build a feeling of closeness and optimism. Kids learn best when they are comfortable with and friendly toward the teacher and each other.

# CHAPTER 10

# The class meeting

The class meeting is the core of the democratic approach to classroom discipline. The meeting consists of time set aside from teaching the curriculum, in which the teacher and the class sit down within a classic meeting structure (chairperson, secretary, agenda, etc.,) to discuss the main issues facing the class. It's the kind of strategy sessions that all groups and organizations have, from companies and governments to committees and social groups.

The class meeting takes on the significance of being the highest decision-making authority in the classroom. Of course, you don't use these class meetings to decide everything. There are some very important aspects of the school day that are already in place, like the curriculum, class hours, and the physical setup of the class. What the meeting does do is allow students to voice their ideas, not about what gets taught but how it gets taught. It also gives them an equal say in how to solve the many issues that crop up in social situations, such as personal problems, social activities and social interest opportunities. And, perhaps most importantly, they are allowed a forum in which they can voice their opinion and feelings.

What the class meeting is not about is to discuss what the teacher has decided on already. The common misconception is that the teacher makes a decision and then calls a "class meeting" to tell everyone about it. On the contrary, the underlying concept of the class meeting is that everyone has to agree to any

# CLASS MEETING Q & A

**PROBLEM:** "I'm worried that the class meetings will take away valuable time I need to spend achieving what I see as my main job – teaching the curriculum."

**ANSWER:** Think of how much time you spend over the year responding to and trying to deal with behavior problems. Now think of how much more time you would have to spend on the curriculum if your class were to be more cooperative. The focus of the class meeting, after all, is to create a cooperative learning environment. This is especially important for students who would normally be disruptive, argumentative, and challenging. The class meeting has been designed to be a powerful tool to be used in your effort to teach the curriculum.

**PROBLEM:** "I'm not comfortable with the idea of sharing power with the students, or even relinquishing it. I guess I just don't have any faith they can handle it without abusing it. Besides, if I loosen my grip on the class, won't the bullies and power kids take over? Won't I be perceived as being weak?"

**ANSWER:** We have learned through experience that when you share power with kids (by giving everyone an equal voice) you are perceived as caring, generous, and understanding rather than weak. What does make you look weak is when the class sees one of their peers getting away with something. When a child breaks a rule and you don't know what to do about it, you look (and are) powerless. Worse, you have no allies – it's you against them. If, on the other hand, you and the class have come up with the rules together, it's up to everyone to see that they are followed. You are not alone nor can you be seen as the one who failed when the rules are broken.

new rule or policy change. That means you have to stop thinking of the class as belonging just to you. When you include your students in the problem-solving/decision-making process, you make it their class as well. When you make the students feel they have some say in how the class is being run, you are adopting an inclusive style of teaching. Although this may sound radical at first, remember that it represents a shift in attitude that is occurring everywhere, including corporations large and small. Don't think of yourself as a maverick by adopting this approach; think of yourself as riding the wave of change that is sweeping through virtually every aspect of our society.

## Using the class meeting for problem solving

Problem solving is just like listening – it's a skill that has to be learned. In the context of the class meeting, problem solving is also about learning how to cooperate. A fundamental psychological truth is that people are much more likely to follow a rule if they have had a hand in forming it themselves. It is, in other words, a cooperative venture. Instead of the teacher dictating the ways things will be, the class is invited to play an active role in decision making. In the past, students obeyed rules mostly out of fear. It worked, in a way. But what it didn't develop was a sense of responsibility and caring in the students. It didn't teach social interest. Today, we want children to follow the rules because they believe it is the right thing to do, not out of fear.

Participating in class meetings is also a great way for students to learn how meetings are conducted, something that will stand them in good stead when they grow up. Being able to lead (not to mention participate) in a meeting is a highly prized and much neglected adult skill. Meetings also teach students how to cooperate, work in teams, problem solve and brainstorm creative ideas. These are just the attributes modern employers are looking for.

## Competition

One of the most important strengths of the class meeting is that it decreases competition. In the autocratically-run class, there is competition to gain favor from the teacher. You can probably remember what it was like when you were a student. Everyone was either vying for the privilege of being the "teacher's pet," or having given up on that, becoming in some way the "rebel without a cause." The autocratic method, with its rewards and punishments, stimulates children to take on these kinds of roles by creating competition. The democratic method (the class meeting) strives to eliminate these roles – to not have good students or bad students. What we do want is a classroom where everyone feels secure and important to the group because of their unique contributions.

In the "real world," people succeed in direct relation to how well they can cooperate – with co-workers, customers, family members, etc. Think of the example of driving – how much cooperation is required to follow the rules of the road and arrive safely to your destination. When cooperation breaks down it is nearly impossible to accomplish your goal and to feel comfortable. Another point to remember is that competition creates a discouraging atmosphere for everyone except those at the very top (and even they have to cope with the stress of staying there). Competition arises between the "smart kids" and the slower ones, between the athletic ones and the ones who aren't, between the "good" students and the "bad". Cooperation fosters a feeling in every member of the classroom that they are valued and accepted.

Cooperation will be higher when we raise their social interest.

## SOCIAL INTEREST

*"In spite of everything, I still believe that people
are really good at heart. Whoever is happy
will make others happy too."*
— ANNE FRANK

Social Interest is a person's ability to have empathy and compassion for others. It is the ability to see a situation as another
person sees it and to understand the emotional impact it
makes on that person's life.

Social interest, the caring and desire to help other people, is
an innate potential. We are all born with this potential. Human
society would not have developed without it. But it must be
nurtured and cultivated. Sadly, the results of a lack of social
interest are all around us – self-centeredness, crime, and a lack
of concern for the environment. Social interest is about developing moral, ethical and spiritual values. Parents play a crucial
role in the child's early years by developing this awareness.

The class meeting provides a wonderful opportunity for your
students to develop social interest by helping the class to
become cooperative. It does this by allowing them to really
hear each other, work together to solve each other's problems,
and cooperate to realize the goals of the classroom. It is, in
other words, an effective forum for bringing them out of
themselves and becoming aware of the fears, aspirations, and
needs of others.

## The first meeting

You may want to start with a preamble that stresses the idea that since this is the first meeting together as a class, you would like to help them achieve their goal of learning. Ask how many people have participated in a class meeting before. If no hands go up, recognize that this will be a new experience for them. Point out that people learn more when they are enjoying themselves and interested in what you are doing. Say something like: "We need to make our first decision together as a class. The purpose of school is to learn, and people always learn more when they are enjoying it. I want to work with you this year to make this a wonderful class, where we will enjoy ourselves. For that reason, I'm interested in our class working together to come up with some ideas of how we want our class to be run this year. This will include planning fun things we can do together like parties and field trips, work projects, and even solving problems we have as individuals and as a class. I've always found that classes that get together and toss around ideas end up to be happier, friendlier places where people learn more. I think you'll find that it will bring us together to share ideas and come up with solutions to our problems."

## Consensus and the "veto"

The class meeting can only work if everyone agrees on the decisions made. That's what makes it democratic. But when people hear the term "democratic," they often immediately think of the political model that involves elections in which the majority rules. But majority rule doesn't work with class meetings. First of all, if the teacher does not agree with the class, she certainly can't go along with the decision. Secondly, if some students don't agree to a rule or a policy, it becomes very difficult, if not impossible, to get their cooperation. They can even undermine the initiative because they are angry and rebellious at being forced. That's why consensus is so important. Consensus means that every one agrees and everyone, including the teacher, has a veto. It is "unanimous rule". The veto means you will never be forced to go along with an idea you are not completely comfortable with.

But how can I achieve consensus, you ask?

If a solution can't be found or a rule agreed upon, the question should be tabled until the next meeting. The students have to think about it that week. If time and brainstorming (see problem solving, chapter 13) don't work, you can break up into small groups or committees. Each group is responsible for coming up with a solution and presenting it to the class. It's important to leave things as they are until a new decision is agreed upon by everyone. Not changing anything until you have achieved consensus means everyone has to put up with the old, unsatisfactory situation until they all agree. If you find it impossible to come up with a solution everyone loves, you can say to the abstainers: "We know this isn't your favorite solution. However, a lot of the others would like to try this. Would you be willing to go along with this for a week and we'll see how it goes."

Even though it's sometimes hard to achieve consensus, it's the only way to insure that everyone works together.

# The agenda

Here is a standard agenda you can use for the basic framework of your meetings. It covers all the essential elements of school life.

1. Things that are going well or have improved (items of encouragement)
2. Classroom planning
3. Classroom jobs (responsibilities)
4. Things that need to be improved (problem solving)
5. Personal problems

## Things that are going well

As we all know, you can only build on strength, not weakness. Unfortunately, studies have shown that students hear a much higher ratio of negative statements about themselves than positive. To correct this and to encourage the modeling of positive attitudes, start off each meeting with recognition and appreciation of what your students have done right during the past week. If you are starting these meetings in midyear and are experiencing more serious problems, talk only about what is going well for the first three or four meetings in order to raise morale.

For problem students, even a tiny change for the better can be beneficial. Some children are not used to hearing nice things being said about them, and you can almost see them shine when it happens.

Here are some examples of what could be discussed:

1. Positive and warm things about each member of the class. Each child can take a turn being the focus of this "positive bombardment." It could go something like this: "My favorite thing about Justin is…."

2. Discuss what has improved over the past week (in particular, talk about problems that were brought up at the last meeting). Again, keep in mind that any improvement at all should be emphasized, because it is such an encouraging tactic.

3. Talk about situations in which students have been helpful to one another. This will be particularly encouraging to students who show sensitivity and thoughtfulness to their peers but are experiencing academic difficulties. In other words, this will illustrate that you are not just interested in academic achievement but social development as well. If you have a student who has shown bullying tactics in the past, it is important to notice and recognize any acts of kindness or thoughtfulness that they may show, no matter how minor. In general, any act of social interest should be

mentioned. It helps change children's behavior by giving them status and recognition for positive behavior rather than negative.

4. Discuss positive values in the class. You can even choose one value, such as honesty, respect, or hard work, and emphasize it during that meeting.

## Classroom planning

This agenda item includes anything from work projects to class outings and field trips. Like the preceding agenda item, this is usually a fun, non-threatening activity that all or most of your students will jump right into.

We often assume that we, as teachers, have to come up with all of the ideas for what the students do, yet many times our best plans backfire. One teacher we know was shocked that her students did nothing but complain about a field trip she worked hard to organize. How can anyone complain about a trip to the zoo? The answer is that they might have felt dictated to, especially older children at the junior high and high school level. It just goes to show how the best of intentions can fail. If you don't involve the students in the plans that affect them, you will not have their full cooperation or enthusiasm.

Here are some things to keep in mind when planning with your students:

1. Give them real choices. Many aspects of school life aren't flexible because of school policies. Having said that, you should still strive to present as many choices as possible to your students. If you can't be flexible about a plan, don't present it as an option for them. For example, the school has a yearly fund-raising BBQ every spring and you would like your students to be involved in the event. Don't pose the question: "Should we have a BBQ this year?" because it's not an option to opt out. Instead, present the (mandatory) event and ask: "How should we as a class participate in the BBQ?" Ask them if they have any of their own creative ideas

about how to participate. Kids need a certain amount of structure, but they also need outlets for their creativity – here is an opportunity for both.

2. Break down into groups (committees). Once you have presented the idea to the whole class and have reached consensus about a project, it is time to plan out the details. Teach your students how to ask the practical questions, such as: Who will do what, when? This gives every student a chance to give their input into the big picture. Once that is done, the bulk of this class planning is best achieved by different (small and workable) groups. In this small group, they can readily see what their role is in the project.

3. Get their input on how to achieve the curriculum goals of their class. Yes, teachers have long seen this as their province. However, students will often work harder and more willingly if they have some say in how their year's work will be done. Obviously what they are going to learn is being decided for them, but you can still use their ideas to find creative ways to cover the material.

We have talked to many teachers that have used this approach. Here are a few examples of student suggestions they have been able to successfully adopt into their lesson plans:

✎ A grade six language arts class acted out a scene from a novel they were studying (videotaping such an activity is an additional option).

✎ One class turned math drills into games (there are lots of them around, and kids are great at dreaming them up).

✎ Some younger students decided to have a Bring Your Pet to School Day at the beginning of the year to help the class get to know each other better.

As creative as children are, be prepared to offer your own suggestions to get the ball rolling if they can't come up with any, especially with younger students.

4. Use the six-step problem-solving method (see Conflict

Resolution, page 158) to break up deadlocks.

5. Let your students know how important and appreciated their contributions are to the class. Try and use encouraging statements like:

- ✎ "Without your ideas, I could never have come up with such a terrific plan."
- ✎ "I find that coming up with the creative ideas is the most difficult part. Thanks for helping."
- ✎ What a great idea. You guys are really working together well. This is going to work out."

## Responsibilities

Just like in a family, responsibilities in a classroom should be shared equally. (In most schools, this really only applies to the elementary years when the students are in the classroom for most or all of the day.) Giving children ongoing responsibilities and getting them to pitch in helps foster group cohesion, build self-esteem, and increase children's respect for their environment. It also teaches them to be more…well, responsible.

Here are some good, open-ended questions that will naturally lead to a discussion about classroom jobs:

- ✎ What jobs do you think we need to do to keep the class running smoothly?
- ✎ What do you think is needed to make our classroom pleasant and well organized?

Once you have established that taking care of the class should be a group effort, you can move on to the idea of working out an equitable system to share the jobs. It's a good idea to rotate the jobs, either weekly or monthly, because some jobs will be more popular than others. (It should be up to the group to decide this, of course.) Together with your students, make a list of all the jobs that need to be done. Ask for volunteers (instead of assigning). If you have more than one person interested in a job, use some sort of fair system for breaking the deadlock, like pulling a name out of a hat.

Here's a list of some jobs that could be considered (use your imagination for more):

- ✎ watering plants
- ✎ emptying garbage cans
- ✎ cleaning sink area
- ✎ cleaning blackboard brushes
- ✎ feeding pets
- ✎ organizing cloakroom (two or more)
- ✎ refilling paper supplies
- ✎ emptying pencil sharpener
- ✎ organizing the bookshelves
- ✎ repairing torn class books
- ✎ collecting milk money
- ✎ taking messages to the office
- ✎ cleaning computer screens

This works best if everyone can do their jobs at the same time every day, although some will be time-sensitive, such as taking the attendance sheet to the office. Together, figure out what the best times are. There should be a visual reference in the classroom that spells out the jobs, who does them, and when. It helps if you use something that can be easily changed. For example, we have seen pockets glued onto a board that had the children's names on them, and names affixed to wooden clothes pegs that can be moved from job to job.

If for some reason the students don't do their jobs, bring it up at the "Things That Need to be Improved" part of the class meeting (see below).

## Things that need to be improved

Of course things never go as smoothly as you would like, and you should be prepared for this agenda item to require the most skill and sensitivity. Examples of problems that are most likely to rear their ugly heads are:

- ✎ Jobs that aren't getting done
- ✎ Students who are having trouble with their schoolwork
- ✎ Homework issues
- ✎ Cliques, bullying, and fighting
- ✎ Communication problems
- ✎ Disrespect (towards teachers or peers)
- ✎ Vandalism
- ✎ Discipline problems (talking out, fooling around, not pay-ing attention, etc.)

The main thing to keep in mind is to always be solution orient-ed. That means the focus must be to work together to improve the situation, not to get someone in trouble. If you have the idea that this is the time to dole out punishments or point out a stu-dent's shortcomings to the others, you can be sure that the stu-dents will be on the defensive and will not work together to find answers in an honest, open way.

Taking responsibility for your mistakes is one of the things you hope to achieve with your students in the class meetings. A good way to do this is to admit them yourself when you have made a mistake. Whenever children hear an adult saying they have made a mistake, it not only makes the adult seem more human in their eyes, but opens the door to their admitting their own mistakes. What is even better is if you acknowledge the mistake and then discuss how you have taken steps to rectify it.

## Defining the problem

During this part of the meeting, problems can be raised by either a student or the teacher. Keep in mind that children will pay more attention to their peers' concerns than to their teacher's. Perhaps you can have a sheet that is posted somewhere that can be used for students to write down (anonymously, if they wish) what problems they would like to see raised at the meeting. During the first few weeks, when you are the sole chairperson, take special care to talk about problems in a sensi-tive way. You can do this by making observations about specific incidents: "I noticed that there was some name calling and put-downs during our volleyball game this week," or "The class seems to be taking a long time to get settled after recess."

## The "why" of the problem

The next question after stating the problem could be to ask if anyone else has noticed it. If you get some hands raised, it makes it easier to proceed to the next step, which is to ask if the class wants to take a few minutes to discuss the problem. Start by asking an open-ended question such as: "Why do you think we have so much name calling during the volleyball games?" Your purpose here is to get everyone looking for the source of the problem. For instance, does it happen when someone makes a mistake, or when we lose a point, or maybe even because we're angry that we're behind? Do people think that bad mouthing the other team is part of the game, or that it is part of creating team spirit? Sometimes children who are raised with a lot of criticism think it's okay to criticize others.

Spending time talking about the problem is time well spent. If you just tell them: "It's wrong, don't do it again," you are simply making a judgment for them, instead of giving them a better understanding of why they do what they do, which is an important part of changing behavior. Emphasis should be directed at the four goals of uncooperative behavior. In this way we are not forming a judgment about an individual student, but exploring the goal. Using active listening techniques to play back children's feelings to them is helpful at this stage (see page 174 for active listening techniques). You can even write the major points on the board and read them back to the class.

## The effects of the problem

Once you've exhausted the discussion on why the problem is happening, ask people how they feel when this (name calling at a game) happens to them. You might get comments like: "I feel angry at the person who said it to me," or "I feel stupid. I feel like quitting."

Throughout this process you have to give the kids encouragement and appreciation for their honesty and openness, and reassure them about how much the class will be helped by this. Let them know they are handling their problems in a very open, courageous, effective, and mature way. Once you've completed the exploration (what they are doing and the impact on others), you can move into finding solutions.

At this point you can either take ideas from the group (something like: "How should we be acting when we get frustrated at a game? How can we handle our emotions when we get excited at a game? What can we do to help us play our best and not hurt each other?"

Now sit back and wait for some good suggestions. Perhaps there will be someone (one of the more sensitive students) who will suggest that the class should encourage each other and not make people feel worse if they make a mistake. Maybe someone will suggest a group cheer at different times of the game. Your job is to restate any ideas that achieve consensus as a new class policy. It might read something like: "From now on, our class will try its best to encourage each other when we're playing sports, by having a team cheer at the beginning and the end, and by not using any put-downs or name calling."

If they don't come up with good ideas, you can of course make your own suggestions. Approach it by saying something like: "I have an idea. Would you like to hear it?" By asking first, it helps them accept your suggestions.

## Using the group – dealing with an academic problem in the class meeting

Many times a teacher is concerned about a child who is working far below his capabilities. After many efforts to encourage this child, he doesn't seem to be making much progress. At this point the teacher may begin to think that perhaps the group might be encouraging to the student, and possibly even help him catch up. If students in the class have demonstrated empathy for others, the teacher might want to bring up his academic problem in a class meeting. However, if the students make fun of each other and use a lot of put-downs, it may not be a good idea.

There are different ways that you can start this process. The least threatening way would be to ask the class how many find math, for example, to be pretty hard this year. There might be a number of children who raise their hand. This particular child sees that he is not alone in having difficulty with the subject. Ask the class some general question about why some students have difficulty with the work. Introduce the idea that lack of confidence and discouragement can cause people to give up. Ask for a show of hands for those who find they tend to give up. If this student raises his hand, which he is most likely to do, we can then move into working with this child in the class meeting.

Methods of encouragement, peer tutoring, and remedial work can begin to help this child. The ideas just discussed may help your students gain some insight. Get them to pull together to combat feelings of discouragement and to resist the tendency to give up when they are behind. Remind them of the importance of working hard and using the resources in the class (their peers, the teacher, computer programs) to catch up.

## Personal Problems

This is the trickiest agenda item for the obvious reasons. A lot of teachers understandably shy away from talking about personal concerns during a group meeting. Teachers' fears range from someone revealing family secrets, to an unleashing of an emotional torrent they can't handle. But in this day and age, we are becoming more open about our problems (as any one who has watched daytime TV will have noticed). Although this may create some discomfort, it also means that many people are no longer forced to carry around corrosive secrets and endure harmful situations. Also, the reality is that most student's common worries are usually much less dramatic than your worst fears: maybe their father is too busy to come to their games, or their dog died, or their grandmother is in the hospital. These are serious problems for them, but nothing that can't be talked about in a classroom to good effect. Besides, sometimes the biggest obstacles to class harmony don't come from the dynamics within the classroom itself, but from stresses in the students' lives.

The main reason for this agenda item is to create more warmth, closeness, and caring within the class. But it is also to reassure children that everyone experiences difficulties, and that the best way to handle problems is to be open and to talk to someone about them. Remember that some children, for a variety of reasons, don't have anyone else they can turn to. If these problems aren't addressed, they can interfere with their ability to learn. Another reason the classroom is a good forum for talking about personal problems is that children can be reassured to learn that their problems are often the same as everyone else's. Finally, words of encouragement from their peers go a lot further than words from an adult.

We know from personal experience how important these meeting revelations can be. While teaching a kindergarten class, one of the students (a five-year old) told us that he was afraid of being alone. "When are you alone?" we asked. "When I get home from school," he replied. It turned out that his 12-year-old sister, who was supposed to be looking after him, was instead going to a friend's house. His working parents were informed and were grateful to find out so they could correct the problem.

To begin this phase of the meeting, explain the parameters of the problems that can be discussed.

> ✎ Don't bring anything into the classroom that might embarrass others. If they think it is something that might not be appropriate or is something they don't want discussed publicly, they should write it down and put it in a

personal problem box so the teacher could read it first.

✎ It should be something they are worried about. The word "worried" will give them a good idea of what this is all about.

✎ Teachers can model appropriate discussion topics by bringing up something in their own life. For example, a teacher going on maternity leave may express how excited she is about having the baby, but also how sad she is that she won't be there to finish the year with her students. This could lead to her and the class arranging for her to visit after the baby is born.

## Using the classroom meeting to diagnose the goals of misbehavior

Children have a remarkable understanding of why their peers misbehave (although not much about their own behavior). This understanding is inherent even at an early age; in fact they are often better at it than adults. That's because adults usually think in terms of causes for misbehavior, while children think in terms of goals. For example, a child would rarely say another child was misbehaving because his mother just had a baby or his parents weren't getting along, but they would say it was because they want attention or they want their own way.

Even though children have a natural bent for this kind of analysis, we don't advise parents to bring up the goals of misbehavior with their children because it often backfires. Their emotional relationship with their children is so close that the children could feel manipulated or psychoanalyzed. But as a teacher, your role is perceived as more emotionally detached. In addition, you are seen as having the role of an educator, so you can approach the teaching of behavior the same as any other subject. The same thing holds true for a counselor. This means that one of the advantages teachers have that parents don't is their role as educators.

### "To change your behavior, you have to first understand it."

One of the best uses of a class meeting is to involve everyone in helping to solve behavioral problems. Bringing up the problem in the meeting helps the child become aware of their behavior and how it affects others. In the class meeting format, you can either talk about a specific child's behavior problem (if the child will allow it), or about the behavior in a more general sense.

Some general misbehavior topics you might want to bring up are: talking, disrupting others, silliness, fighting, put-downs and general disrespect.

Here are the steps for dealing with a behavioral problem in the class meeting:

- ✎ State the problem clearly and simply ("There have been a lot of disruptions when I'm trying to teach.")
- ✎ Ask if anyone else has noticed the problem.
- ✎ Start to investigate why this is happening. ("Does anyone have any ideas as to why people are talking when I'm trying to teach?") You are trying to get the students to articulate the goals of misbehavior ("Maybe people don't want to do that subject, they would rather have fun." This is a classic power goal).
- ✎ Ask how people in the class feel when these disruptions occur. You can add your feelings too, but use the "I" message format (see page 180).
- ✎ Ask the class for solutions to the problems. All solutions should be written down. Make sure you follow through with whatever has been decided

If someone is willing to talk about their behavior problem, deal with it in the same way. Use the "disclosing the goal" process (see page 58). Emphasize that, once the goal has been discovered, the entire class will help the student to overcome the need to achieve the goal through disruptive means, and help her find cooperative ways to achieve significance.

# Meeting nuts and bolts

## The physical setup

Ideally, the meeting is held in a circle. This is the most inclusive, egalitarian way for everyone to sit, especially since it doesn't put the teacher or anyone else at the "head" of the meeting. It also allows for everyone to see each other easily. Of course, it may be time consuming to put 30 chairs into a circle, so you could consider sitting in a circle on the floor, or (if possible) having a spare room set up just for meetings.

## The chairperson

The chairperson's job is essentially to lead the meetings by keeping order, following the agenda, and recognizing the person who's turn it is to speak. Naturally, the teacher will chair the meetings for the first five or six times, just to show everyone how it's done. After that, it's time for the students to run the meetings (with the teacher as an active and equal participant). Let go of the reins gradually, but as a general rule, the sooner the better.

Participating in a well-run meeting is a fantastic opportunity for your students to learn leadership qualities. In fact, this is a great way for children of all ages to learn how to run a meeting, something that will prove invaluable when they take their place in the adult world. Before your students take the reins, prepare a short lesson on what the job entails.

The chair should rotate after every meeting so that everyone gets a chance. You might also want to have a co-chair, who would act as a recorder to jot down the minutes. You may select the chair yourself and you should encourage everyone to participate, but don't force anyone – that wouldn't be democratic. You could ask the class to come up with ways to select the chairperson for every meeting. The main idea is to come up with a way that doesn't hurt anyone's feelings. For example, you could suggest pulling names out of a hat. This simple method is probably the best way because it not only includes everyone, it's also the fairest. Another way is to ask them to volunteer and then make up a chart for the year.

Here is a list of the attributes and responsibilities of a good chairperson:

- ✎ To be respectful to all students in the class. To treat them the way they would like to be treated.
- ✎ To be encouraging. You can show your students how to do it by being encouraging yourself.
- ✎ To make sure the agenda has been followed.
- ✎ To make sure that the rules pertaining to the meeting that were set up by the group are followed.
- ✎ To keep the flow of the meeting going.
- ✎ To enforce the "no put-downs" rule.
- ✎ To make sure that only those recognized by the chair speak, and that they speak with no interruptions.
- ✎ To make sure the meeting starts and ends on time.

## Other Jobs

*Time Keeper.* This student's job is to carefully time each segment on the agenda to make sure it doesn't drag on (this keeps people from wasting time or drifting off).

*Recorder.* Keeps a record of all decisions passed by the class.

One of the big worries teachers have is letting the more obstreperous students lead the meetings. Won't they take the opportunity to ruin the meeting? Won't they immediately abuse the position and power? Well no, actually, they probably won't. For one thing, being at the center of attention and in control is just where these children who crave attention and power want. Besides, it's good for them to have to maintain order. It gets them behaving in a completely different way and seeing things from a completely different side.

If they do act out, however, it then becomes everyone's

responsibility to see that the rules of the class meeting are followed. If the chair is messing up, it is up to the class to remind her that it is her responsibility to conduct the meeting.

Make sure everyone agrees beforehand on what the chair can and cannot say when maintaining order during the meeting. Respect must be given by the chair to the students at all times. If the chairperson needs to regain order, he can say something like: "Jim, we agreed that no one talks out of turn."

## Duration

Ideally the class meeting would last at least one hour and be held at least once a week, but since that may be too much time for many teachers to take from the curriculum, a half hour meeting will do just fine. For the lower grades (kindergarten and grade one) where attention spans are lower, three, 20-minute meetings a week is best, although we have had successful half-hour meetings with first graders (their high excitement level kept them tuned in).

Some people wonder what the class will talk about for one hour, but that is never a problem. In fact, you will wish you had more time because there is so much to discuss.

Having meetings only now and then will dilute the experience of expressing and listening to problems and their possible solutions. The idea of the class meeting – and the democratic give and take it represents – is something that has to be incorporated into the student's school life. If it is reinforced on a regular basis, the meeting will become the first thing a student thinks of when presented with a problem. If you don't have regular meetings, the danger is that situations will arise which, if they aren't handled immediately, will persist or escalate and be much tougher to solve later.

## Dealing with disruption during the meeting

Assume that everyone will participate in the meetings. However, if you have a student that is really into power and doesn't want to participate, don't force them. They can sit out and do some reading or other activity that doesn't disturb the meeting.

It is just as important to keep order during the class meeting as any other time of the day. If their rebellion takes the shape of disrupting the meeting, give the Go Signal (page 47).

# CHAPTER 11

# The problem student

A s any teacher knows, children are extremely social. The relationships between the students in your class are a result of each student's viewpoint of themselves and of their peers. If a child feels inadequate when socializing, for example, his behavior will reflect that. He might become withdrawn and isolated, or he might react violently with bullying tactics. Whatever the case, children play different, usually destructive roles (destructive to themselves or others) when they are feeling negative. This is never good for the group.

The purpose of this chapter is to explain how to understand the purpose of the different socially unacceptable behaviors that can occur in a classroom. Only then can you rectify the problem and maintain order in the class without inadvertently trampling over the self-esteem of the offending student.

## Withdrawal

Sometimes withdrawal stems from a lack of social interaction from a very early age, or because the child has had very negative and discouraging encounters with adults or peers. They may have been rejected or humiliated, verbally or even physically abused. Some children have introverted temperaments and will withdraw to avoid the pressure of social demands.

## Purpose:

The withdrawing child could be trying to achieve any one of the four goals:

1. Attention – How nice it is to have all the children asking you to come and play, which they will often do for a withdrawn child, at least at first. If he eventually gives in and rejoins the group, you can bet attention was his goal.
2. Power – He wants to do his own thing. If he withdraws, he can choose what he wants. He doesn't have to bend or subordinate himself to anyone. He becomes strong and in control in his isolation.
3. Revenge – This may be his way of coping after being hurt in some way. By withholding his attention, he is making a statement to the group. In fact, he is himself rejecting the group. The posture here is one of disdain or outright indifference: "You're not good enough for me."
4. Assumed Inadequacy – His feelings of inferiority make him feel he will not be able to make friends, or that he doesn't have the skill to play games with any facility. By withdrawing, he doesn't have to risk failure.

## The behavior

Whatever the reason for the withdrawal, the movement of the one that withdraws is away from the other children. For instance, the withdrawn child will enter the playground by himself and avoid joining any of the groups. That could be because he might not understand the social play cues that most people know instinctively. Or he doesn't know how to approach or enter a group of children, so he merely hangs back and observes. He will have a cautious, guarded demeanor, the opposite of some of the children who will look happy and relaxed at their play. When they are with others they are suffering psychological pain. It could be a form of anxiety or depression or a fear of others. What they fear is that others will look down on them, that's because they are often very self-critical.

It is important to understand that the withdrawn child has given up trying to interrelate. This is not to be confused with the shy child. Shy children can very well have some tendency to withdraw and be awkward in groups, but they will also have at least one friend. The withdrawn child, on the other hand, is an isolate (see Sociometry, chapter 15).

Withdrawal is usually not that much of a behavioral problem because the child is usually not acting out. But that doesn't mean it's alright. In fact, the withdrawn child is much more deeply discouraged then the acting out child. Because they tend to not share their thoughts with others, we often don't know how much they are suffering inwardly and therefore we tend to overlook this problem.  It's not too much to say that, as human beings, our prime goal is to feel connected to the group. The withdrawn child needs your help in finding his place.

## Solutions

Helping the withdrawn student can start the first day of school by including them in the social integration exercises listed in The First Day (Chapter 9). Basically you want to give them opportunities to socialize and be a part of the group in some way. This can be facilitated by pairing the child off with someone you think might be suitable as a friend, someone who is popular but not critical (see Sociometry, chapter15, for ways of finding suitable partners). This friendly partner could sit near them, tutor them, or just simply be friendly with them. Having the withdrawn child participate in smaller groups for projects, or even being in charge of projects, can also be a less intimidating way for them to ease into a social situation. They can even participate in playtime with younger children that might not be as intimidating as their peers.

The teacher can be instrumental in opening up the withdrawn child. Make yourself available. Make a concerted effort to give them a lot of eye contact and always be open, friendly, and inviting. Engage them in discussions often, especially if you think they are prone to daydreaming, which makes it all too easy for them to withdraw into a world of their own making. Stand close to them so you keep their attention, and ask them a lot of questions (out of your interest in them as people) that don't have right or wrong answers, always listening carefully to what they say, and responding to it. All of this might be easier than you think because withdrawn children are often more comfortable with adults.

Teach them the little social tricks for opening social doors and greeting people ("Hi. Can I play too?" "Can I play next?") Most importantly, be positive and encouraging. Let the child know you think they can and will make friends, that they are worthy and likable. Let them know you will help them accomplish this. Teach them problem solving skills and help them learn appropriate ways of becoming friends with someone. Encourage them to join volunteer groups within the school, or outside groups like the Scouts, Girl Guides, soccer, or theatre programs.

It's also your job to include them at class time, calling on them for answers, for example. Make sure the group sees you asking them questions and assigning jobs to them, especially those that involve forms of communication such as delivering messages. Make sure the class sees the positive side of this child; this could include putting their work up on the bulletin board or asking them to participate in news. What the teacher shouldn't do is put this child in any social situation where he may feel stressed or embarrassed.

# Aggressive behavior – The bully

### The behavior

Bullying is one of the most repugnant behavioral problems, for both teachers and students. With stories about school violence like Columbine being splashed across the front pages, more and more schools are trying to deal with bullying and school violence with a strong hand. Everything from police presence and metal detectors to zero tolerance is being tried.

The only thing that is not being tried is to understand the causes of bullying so that we could try to deal with the roots of the problem, not just the symptoms.

Essentially, bullying occurs when a person inflicts injury or discomfort on another person. Verbal bullying comes in the form of threats, degradation, and teasing, while physical bullying involves everything from hitting, kicking, and pushing to vandalizing property and making rude gestures.

Bullying can be carried out by an individual or a group against one person, or even another group. But in order to be considered true bullying there has to be a power imbalance in which the bully is more powerful. Also, in order for an action to be considered bullying, there has to be no provocation on the part of the victim. Bullies appear to have no empathy or compassion for those they trample on.

The question we are often asked is: "Why do these kids, often from seemingly good homes, turn into bullies?" We believe that the causes are usually not genetic but stem primarily from influences of the family environment, and that the discipline methods of the family are major factors in this development. Having said that, we also think there are other influences that have a role, such as peer groups, the constant violence that is offered by television, movies and video games, and even the child's unique interpretations of the vagaries of life.

One study carried out over a 22-year period revealed that aggressiveness is handed down from generation to generation. Parents who used severe punishment as discipline were a model for violent behavior. This parenting style is based on a basic inconsistency in which a particular behavior is happily permitted one day and severely punished the next, depending on the parent's mood. Because of this inconsistency, children learned that the punishment they received was not the result of what they did, but rather the outcome of their parent's mood. Living in this kind of unpredictable environment where there is no appreciable connection between cause and effect, creates a feeling of vulnerability and anxiety.

## The bully's inner justification

The bully's goal of power and revenge is better understood in light of the above influences. By exerting power, control, and manipulation, a bully can order his world to protect himself against others who he feels could violate him. In other words, the bully believes the outer world carries the same threats and inconsistencies as his family. (This kind of response can be amplified by the bully's peer group if he is teased and rejected by them – a particularly explosive situation.) If he has the upper hand, he wrongly reasons, people will be afraid to challenge him. Being essentially a frightened person, the bully is always sensitive to possible threats, and perceives others to be the enemy. This is his justification for his aggressive actions. If he can successfully justify these actions to himself, the bully doesn't have to suffer the pains of shame or guilt, and therefore does not have to demonstrate compassion or empathy for his victims, believing that they deserved what they got.

Bullies start fights with little or no provocation. The other children are understandably afraid of them, and don't want the bullies as their friends. Ironically, bullies usually see themselves as innocent and this unfriendliness as hostility. They can thus become even more isolated and alienated.

One characteristic of the bully is that the solution to their relationship problems is always to fight. When children make a mistake, such as bumping into them by accident, it is perceived as an affront, and the reaction is hostility. The bully doesn't want to give the other person the benefit of the doubt. In fact, he looks for opportunities to interpret hostility in others, which give him justification for striking back. When others become angry with him and strike back, the bully is honestly puzzled, saying: "What did I do?"

If the bully is anti-authority, and if he manages to attract loyal followers, he can cause havoc in the classroom, in effect bullying the teacher and the entire class. They can be so persistent and nasty and even physically threatening that they can actually drive a teacher out. We have heard of kids bragging that "teachers don't last long with us." If you're not lucky, you can have two or three subgroups (or gangs) openly or subtly warring for dominance in your class.

The bullying behaviors of young children are the prototypes of the delinquency in teenagers and the criminal activities of adulthood. In one study it was found that 60% of the bullies in grades six to nine were involved in criminal behavior by the time they reached age 24. The inference here is that they seem to carry on their bullying behavior into their adult years, and possibly perpetrate it upon their own families. We have to put a stop to this cycle of bullying. For every bully we help in our schools, there will be one more generation of children growing up in emotionally healthy and safe environments.

## How big is the bullying problem?

Various studies indicate that anywhere from 8% to 18% of school children experience being bullied once a week or more. Approximately 6% of the school children are classified as bullies. This means that there is on the average one bully for every class of 20 children. In this same class, two children are bullied frequently. That means that one out of seven (15%) students in a class of 20 are either victims or victimizers. It's not hard to imagine that children trying to work in an environment of intimidation will find it difficult to learn. Here are some of the more salient points that have appeared in related research over the past ten years about the phenomenon of bullying:

✎ In general, bullies tend to be boys, but female bullies are on the increase. Our culture depicts power and strength as the masculine ideal. However, it's now becoming increasingly common for girls to do strenuous workouts, partly just to get fit, but also to bulk up, or simply as a way of becoming more powerful, either for self-protection or for bullying others.

✎ When girls bully, it is less physical but more apt to be something like malicious gossip, the spreading of rumors, and the manipulation of friendships, but there is also strong evidence of girls belonging to gangs and using violence against other girls.

✎ The five highest rationalizations for boys involved in bullying were that their victims: "didn't fit in", "were physically weak," "were short-tempered," or that it depended on: "who their friends were" and "the clothes they wore."

✎ Girls were motivated to bully when others: "didn't fit in," "didn't look right," "cried or were too emotional," "were overweight," or "had good grades."

✎ Bullies look for victims who are unable to defend themselves, and also those who are looked down upon by society and the media. Sometimes bullies get support from other children since the victims may not be accepted and liked, and these others may even join in the bullying.

✎ Two-thirds (66%) of children with special educational needs are bullied, which is far more often than mainstream students (10%). Being perceived as different, or not as good, often makes children a target for bullies.

✎ Bullies frequently target children who are smaller, hypersensitive, unhappy, cautious, anxious, quiet, or withdrawn. These children are generally passive and nonassertive, and tend to react to bullying by crying and withdrawing when attacked.

✎ One-third of the students admitted that they would join others in bullying a child they didn't like. This is an indication that there are more children who lack the compassion and empathy than was thought. These children are unwilling to take a stand against aggression and will join others in bullying in order to fit in, even if they know it is wrong. Remember, evil can only exist when good people do nothing.

✎ Most students who were bullied told someone about their experience, most often their friends, followed by parents, teacher, principal, and a counselor. Approximately half of the students who told someone about the experience claimed it made the situation better. About one out of 10 students said that telling someone else made it worse. Most students said that they would tell someone if they were bullied daily. This is a strong indication that by verbalizing their problem to others, children feel that things will improve.

✎ The majority of the students felt they could defend themselves if they were bullied. If students have confidence in their ability to handle bullying, not only by fighting back but being able to verbalize effectively, the problem would decrease.

✎ About 75% of the students felt like hurting or upsetting another student sometimes or often. This would indicate that most children have very poor skill development in dealing with social problems.

✎ About 50% of the students said that they had bullied another student as part of a group during the year. 20% said that they bullied others frequently when they were part of a group. With those kinds of numbers, it's no wonder that there are so many problems in classrooms.

✎ About a third of the students said they would be interested in talking about the problem of bullying so that something could be done about stopping it.

✎ About one-third of the teachers said that bullying was a serious problem for them.

✎ The majority of teachers felt that talking about bullying was a good way to solve the problem. Other suggestions included raising children's self-esteem, assertiveness, and respect for others.

## Interventions for bullying

Silence about bullying is tantamount to accepting it. What makes inaction even worse is that this is a problem that can be resolved. However, some solutions only treat the symptoms without getting to the root of the problem.

Zero tolerance is one of the latest and most popular methods for dealing with bullying and violence. With zero tolerance, a student is expelled for any and all acts of aggression or bullying. This is an easy answer to a very disturbing problem – in some ways too easy because it is really only a temporary solution. Yes, it does send a clear message to the bullies, and it also gives immediate relief and protection to the victims, but let's look at both the immediate and long-term results of this policy.

One of the negative results of expelling bullies is that they can carry their aggression to other venues in the community. We have removed them from the school but we haven't changed their attitude, given them problem-solving skills, or taught them compassion and empathy. Zero tolerance helps bullies justify their anti-social actions. And, even though they are removed from the social group of the school, bullies can and frequently do form their own groups, or join gangs where their aggressive behavior will give them status and belonging. Society deals (at great expense) with their behavior in the courts, but the children who have been victimized by them are left with lifelong physical and emotional scars.

What would be more helpful than zero tolerance in the long term, both for the bully and society at large, would be preventative measures, such as better parenting, making life skills a part of the curriculum, and dealing with bullying as and when it happens in the class meetings.

## Prevention

### 1. Class Meetings

In the class meeting, the bully has a real chance to develop empathy and hear how their actions affect others, while making them a de facto part of the group. The meetings are also a great place to give them encouragement, and bullies need encouragement to counteract their feelings of inadequacy. Although it may appear that they feel superior, their constant need to prove themselves indicates vast feelings of self-doubt. People who are comfortable with themselves and have great self-esteem don't have anything to prove.

Another reason to include bullies in class meetings is that they are often ostracized, isolated, and suffer from a lack of social interest. Every opportunity must be taken to find their talents and utilize them for the benefit of the group. Realistically it could take months or even years to turn someone like this around, but be patient. Keep telling yourself that anyone this young has the potential for change. The idea here is to avoid labeling anyone "the bad kid." The other students will also learn a lot about problem-solving, consequences and motivation, by working with the bully in the class.

Because bullies mistakenly perceive others as their enemy, they need help to view others positively and cooperate with the group. Great pains must be taken to not antagonize the bully or make it look like anyone is ganging up on him.

## 2. Parent Study Groups – Teaching Parenting Skills

Parents have by far the most impact on a child's development. It's unrealistic, therefore, to talk about preventing children's behavioral problems without including parents. What we need is nothing less than a campaign to help parents learn the essential skills they need in order to help their children develop social interest. This is an idea that is gaining momentum as people begin to understand that parenting involves much more than just loving children and providing the basics of life. We tend to blame parents when their children are a problem, but this blame needs to be replaced with the realization that, although parents do the best job they can, most of them have never had (or seized) the opportunity to learn the skills needed for this most difficult job. Today however, because of the huge amount of media attention and discussion about parenting, there is no stigma attached to attending a class or reading a book on the subject. In other words, we now see it as a skill that should be studied and mastered rather than something that necessarily comes naturally.

It is not enough for teachers to tell parents that their child is a problem, they must be able to offer practical help. Every school should provide a study group for any parent who is interested, particularly those whose children are having behavioral problems. Without it, they may continue to inflame the aggression of their children by the severity of their discipline.

Here is what typically happens:

The parents of a problem child are constantly getting calls from the school telling them how bad their child is.

*School:* "*Mrs. Smith? Johnny is in the office again for fighting. We think you had better come and pick him up again and talk to him.*"

*Parent:* "*But this is the third time this month. Why are you sending him home to me? I don't know what to do with him. Why can't you discipline him?*"

*School:* "*That's what we're trying to do, Mrs. Smith. But we want you to follow through with him at home. It's really your job to discipline him.*"

This game of Ping-Pong that goes on between the school and the parents, with the child as the ball, goes on a lot. But the irony is, it's both their jobs. Parent study groups, backed by the school, are one way to connect home and school. They offer an empathetic and supportive place for parents to turn when they are experiencing problems with their children. In fact, we believe that all parents of school age children should participate in a parent study group.

### 3. Adopting a curriculum which includes social living

We spend almost all of the time in schools teaching our students facts and methodologies, but almost no time on how to be successful people. We teach them academic skills but not life skills. The fundamentals of a democratic society need to be reinforced through the curriculum of the school. Included in that are the life skills needed in order to treat others with respect while maintaining self-respect. Simply put, the curriculum needs to go beyond the three "R's." It should be expanded to include things like: anger management, conflict resolution techniques, respect for self and others, communication, leadership, and even encouragement skills so that they can understand why people do what they do and be able to help themselves and each other when they are confronted with difficult situations.

# The extreme attention getter

## The Behavior

You'll be able to pick this student out the first day. Usually bold and appearing self-confident, they will walk into your class for the first time, look you right in the eye, and start talking. They are the ones that get noticed, whose names you know well by the end of the first day.

The extreme attention getter is often the classic "class clown" who will do just about anything to gain the spotlight, from falling off of a chair to picking their nose and doing creative things with the result. If left to their own devices, extreme attention getters would dominate the class and everyone in it.

## The Purpose

This is an extreme example of the goal of undue attention we talked about in chapter 5. It's typical of someone who only feels significant or in a "plus position" when receiving attention.

They are, in fact, very "needy" people that only feel complete or significant with the help of others' attention. For that reason, they feel the need to be recognized by others virtually all of the time – sometimes every few minutes.

Like all misbehavior this kind of behavior reveals a lack of social interest. To ask others to pay attention to you all the time is to ignore the fact that they have things to do besides marveling at your antics.

Sometimes this kind of student can be so disruptive that they can't be in the class at all, and are either sent to the office or to a special behavioral class.

## Solutions

Your main focus should be on helping these children become more independent, to not feel they have to rely on others for their significance. For that reason, it's very important to not give them the attention they are seeking when they misbehave. If their behavior gets the desired payoff (which is attention), it will of course continue. Since understanding the motivation (the unconscious goal) is the key to helping these students, it's also important to involve the child himself in the solution. Try and find out together what the purpose behind all this clowning around could be. This is a good time to use a one-on-one with the child to help them discover the goal. In a supportive, inclusive manner, state what the problem is and ask indirect, open-ended questions.

*Teacher: "John, I have noticed that there are a lot of times in the day that I have to speak to you and remind you to get back to work. Usually it's because you are talking to your friends or not paying attention to me when I'm giving instructions."*

*John: "Uh huh?"*

*Teacher: "You don't sound like you agree. Can we talk about this for a few minutes?"*

*John:* "Yeah, I guess so."

*Teacher:* "Good. So tell me, how do you feel things are going in the class?"

*John:* "Well, things are fine, but I guess I'm getting into a little bit of trouble sometimes."

*Teacher:* "What kind of trouble?"

*John:* "You know, like you said. You get mad at me sometimes for fooling around. And sometimes I get a detention."

*Teacher:* "And how do you feel when you get into trouble?"

*John:* "I don't like it. But I don't think it's fair. I'm just trying to have fun. I'm just fooling around."

*Teacher:* "That is interesting. Do you have any ideas about why you like to fool around so much?"

*John:* "I don't know."

*Teacher:* "Do you mind if I make a few guesses?"

*John:* "Okay."

The teacher goes though the list of possible goals, starting with the one you think is most likely to be the right one, in this case, undue attention seeking.

*Teacher:* "Could it be that you enjoy being the center of attention?"

Sometimes the student will agree with you if you really have hit the nail on the head, but sometimes they will avoid giving a truthful answer. We often don't want to reveal our unconscious goal and have it out in the open. In this case, John says no but gives a small smile and turns away slightly. (As we have said, this is known as a recognition reflex. His body language shows that you are correct, even though he has denied it.)

*Teacher:* "Well John, you said no, but your smile said that your answer really is yes."

*John: (with a sheepish grin) "Maybe."*

*Teacher: "So you like people to remember that you're there. You like it when people pay attention to you. I understand that, and I'd like to figure out a way to give you the attention you want in a way that won't stop the other kids from learning or me from teaching. That way you can have the attention you like, but you won't be getting into so much trouble."*

Now you ask, in a way that shows you are genuinely interested, how many times a day he thinks he needs attention from you. Ten times a day? Twenty? Take whatever he says – let's say it's fifteen. The next day when he acts up or otherwise causes you to pay attention to him, say: "OK John, that's one." When it happens again say "John, two." And so on.

This is called "spitting in their soup." John is getting the attention he craves, but he is not enjoying it. That's because once you have brought the unconscious goal to the surface and allowed him to recognize it, the game is up. It's only fun and fulfilling when it's unconscious.

Soon, you can ask John if he thinks you could lower the number of times he needs the attention, perhaps ten or even five times would suffice. Of course, by now John is starting to become annoyed with the constant reminders. That's alright. What you are doing is making him aware of what he is doing and why, but you are doing it without damaging the teacher-student relationship.

When you have an extreme attention getter, it's not enough for only the teacher to work with the child; you need the help of the whole class. Expect to spend a lot of time working on this problem. Specifically, you have to persuade the others in the class to not give the attention getter any attention (keep in mind that this has to be done in a very supportive way). Ask John if he would mind it if you brought this up at a class meeting so everyone could help him solve the problem. This is a delicate situation and the utmost sensitivity must be used. John has to feel sure that both you and the class will be supportive. (This can only be done after you have taught the class all about the four goals of misbehavior, so that the discussion has been put firmly into an educational context.) If he says no, you can bring it up with the class as a general discussion without mentioning him. If he agrees, bring it up at a class meeting by describing the problem, discussing why he might be doing it, and asking the class to help him. You want the class to come up with their own valid reasons why this is harmful, not just for them, but for the attention getter as well. Use the open-ended questioning style to stimulate discussion. Here are examples of good questions to ask:

- ✎ "What happens when John acts up?"
- ✎ "Why do you think he does this?"
- ✎ "How do you react when he gets your attention?"
- ✎ "How does this affect the work we're trying to do in the class?"
- ✎ "How does it feel when you are interrupted while working?"

If this results in any negative feelings being expressed about John, the teacher has to ask: "If John stopped doing this, would you still feel annoyed with him?"

Almost always the answer will be no. To inject a note of encouragement at this stage, you could ask the class to come up with things they like about John. This stresses that people like John, just not his attention getting. It separates "the deed" from the doer."

Then you can respond with something like: "We all want our classroom to work well so we can accomplish what we are here to do. I would like to be able to teach without being interrupted. So we all need to help John make some changes."

Now the problem-solving phase begins.

Essentially, you want the class to stop reacting in *any* way to John's antics.

Perhaps the class could come up with an agreed-upon signal or phrase to be given when someone gives him attention, but nothing of a put-down nature. It would make matters worse if the class turned against him.

You also want students to remind John, in a nice way, that he is disturbing everyone.

In general, it's important to be encouraging to attention getters when they do work on their own and keep out of everyone else's hair. Say things like, "I noticed how well you managed your time this morning."

Find ways for them to constructively channel their need for the attention of others. We once met a former teacher of a very famous comedian. She had taken one of our teacher's workshops and told us about what an extraordinary class clown the comedian was (he still is, only now he earns $20 million per movie for doing it). Her solution was to promise him 15 minutes of performance time in front of the class at the end of the day as long as he had managed to not disturb anyone. Not only did this work, but when producers of a TV biography on him asked for the name of his favorite teacher to interview, he gave them her name.

This can be done with any student, just by having them read their work aloud to the class. It's also important to put them into helpful roles so that they begin to receive their significance by helping others instead of distracting them. Give them lots of jobs to do. Let them tutor others. Encourage them to join the drama club or play sports.

# The Rebel

## The Behavior

Remember the famous 1950's "biker" film, The Wild One with Marlon Brando? There is one scene in which someone asks the Brando character, who is the leader of a motorcycle gang, a question: "What are you rebelling against, Johnny?" To which Brando replies: "What have you got?" The rebel always hates everything.

## The purpose

The rebel is into power, the second goal of misbehavior. There is a deep-seated anger always bubbling below the surface. They feel they should be free to do anything they want (without understanding the ramifications of everyone acting this way). They are doing it because they want to feel strong and in control. Of course they will want to resist you, but you can't fight them. You have to somehow get the rebel on your side.

## Solutions

The best strategy is to get them involved in activities and situations in which they can gain achievement. One way to do this is to encourage them to participate in sports and clubs. Accomplishments always produce a feeling of achievement, which is very important for the rebels because it gives them a feeling of strength, knowledge and power. They don't want to be looked upon as being stupid or vulnerable.

One of the best things to do with a rebel is to put them in a leadership role, especially if it can be one that is normally occupied by the teacher. For example, make them the one responsible for calling the class to attention. Have them tutor other students in a subject they are strong in. That way, they are using their leadership abilities to help you or others, while still feeling they are in some way in charge and not under your thumb.

Another strategy it to disarm them. Suppose a rebellious student informs you that they "hate French." If you come back with something like, "You're wrong. You have to take French. Just do it," you've lost them. Instead, surprise and disarm them by acting interested. "Thank you for telling me, I didn't know. What can we do about this?" What you don't want to do is engage in a power struggle with them so that they dig in their heels.

Rebels think that people who follow the rules are weak. They believe that if you follow the rules the authority figures have control over you, which shows you are afraid of authority. Your job is to reframe the concept of rules for them. You have to convince them that people who follow rules are making a choice. They are doing it of their own free will. Bring this up at a class meeting. Point out that people follow rules and cooperate with others because they can see that the rules are necessary in order to make life easier. It's not because they are weak, it's because they can see that the rules make sense and give us freedom within limits.

# Cliques

A clique is an exclusive group that sees itself as an elite. They are generally very hard to break into. Cliques are all about being superior, and one sure way to elevate yourself to a superior position is to put down those around you. For this reason, cliques tend to be viewed by others as exclusive.

Cliques are formed around common interests – sports, fashion, the arts, social scenes, even things like drugs, or antisocial behavior. Children understand the hierarchy of these groups – "That's the popular clique," or, "Those are the tough kids." Some are even formed by a group of undesirable children with whom no one wants to be part of.

In some ways, cliques provide a few of the positive things that gangs provide; things like belonging, power, and status. The problem with cliques is their exclusivity. Not belonging to these cliques, being one who is not fast enough, or good looking enough, or bad enough, can cause children to really suffer and feel ostracized.

The big trouble with cliques is that they are seen by a lot of teachers as some kind of benign club, and many a blind eye has been turned toward them. But cliques can cause a great deal of isolation and loneliness because of their very exclusivity. Cliques can also be the source of a great deal of put-downs, teasing, and torment. If it reaches this stage, the clique is engaging in bullying. This can be much more devastating to the victim because the clique has the power of a group, often a very popular group.

For anyone working toward an egalitarian, democratic school atmosphere, cliques present a solid obstacle. Their very existence creates a class system. The social world of students, especially at the high school level, doesn't tolerate diversity very well and cliques just amplify this problem.

## Busting the Cliques

Clique busting is not about destroying friendships, it's about removing the rigid fences that are built around group membership. It is, in microcosm, about breaking down the barriers of a class society. Here are some ways you can diminish the power of the cliques in your class, and build up acceptance of the differences that make life interesting.

- Create opportunities for interaction with non-clique members. You can do this by encouraging clique members to work on different teams, committees, and projects with non-clique students. Try having them do a mural together, assist the coach of the volleyball team, or do the PR for an upcoming dance.
- Since they are often popular, try and pair clique members with students who are withdrawn, need help with a subject, or are new to the class.
- Leadership training provides the opportunity for clique members to learn better social skills and a greater acceptance of diversity.
- Don't turn a blind eye to any group of students ganging up on an individual to tease or taunt.
- Use conflict resolution techniques if there is a conflict between groups.
- Show the way yourself by never showing favoritism. Lots of kids complain that the popular students are treated preferentially.
- When it's appropriate (in class meetings or conflict resolution situations), talk openly about cliques and why they can be harmful.

✎ If you see someone associating with someone outside their clique, or even two groups doing something together, comment favorably on it.

# CHAPTER 12

# Academic problems

As a general rule, students who don't do well academically suffer from low self-esteem – they truly believe they can't do it. They feel that they are less capable than others and they come to this conclusion by comparing themselves to their classmates and siblings. Other sources of low self-esteem are negative messages from home and school, in addition to poor academic performance. Of course, it's a bit like the "chicken and the egg" scenario – what comes first, the low self-esteem or the poor performance that can cause or reinforce poor self-image? What we do know is that getting a poor evaluation, like a poor grade or negative comment on written work, lowers the self-esteem of both the students who do well and those that are struggling. The latter group often doesn't even see the point in the work they are forced to learn. ("When will I ever need to use logarithms in my life?")

This lack of confidence can be so all-encompassing that it is very difficult to change their belief system. Some are deficient in just one or a few subjects, while others are deficient in all of them. This last group tends to trigger the alarm bells, and often they are sent to special education classes. There are pros and cons to this approach. Those that approve of it say it allows for special attention to be given to the child. Those opposed (and this is an increasing number) say it tends to make the student feel singled out for being stupid, while in a regular class, the child will at least feel relatively normal and perhaps have more hope.

Students that are doing poorly in a subject are usually embarrassed about it and are therefore very good at masking it to avoid detection. For the same reason, they are reluctant to ask for help. But primarily, these students have given up because they believe that no matter how hard they try or how much help they receive, they won't be able to turn it around.

## Understanding the child

If a child has given up, it means that progress is almost impossible until you can succeed in changing their self-view. You have to make them believe they really can do it. The first step is in understanding the child. Resist what is often the first response of an adult – to give the standard "hard work" lecture: "You have to buckle down and work harder at this. You need to do an extra hour at night and really concentrate." You're right, of course. As a teacher, you are very good at looking at the problem and seeing the solution. But that's not going to do you any good here, because you are putting the cart before the horse. The child is not ready to hear what she has to do yet. To help convey the idea that you understand what she is going through and to create nonjudgmental rapport with her, say things like: "It sounds to me that you are feeling you will never be able to understand this work," or "you feel you are so far behind there is no way you can catch up. You really feel discouraged."

## Build a plan together

Human beings always feel tremendous relief when someone demonstrates understanding regarding their problems and themselves. You have now established a closer rapport, which opens the door to helping them. Once you discover where their areas of weakness are, you can start doing whatever remedial work is necessary. At the same time, you have to always be using encouragement techniques. Let them know that even though they don't think they can do it, you are convinced they can. You are going to work on it together and you will positively not give up on them. You have to genuinely believe they can do it – this is crucial. You can't fake this. There have been studies done that prove how powerful the teacher's expectations are. For example, they found that when a teacher was told a student was gifted, the student performed better, and did poorly if the teacher was told they were slow.

The next step is to get them to commit to trying for at least a short period of time (a week or two). Don't forget, at this stage they still aren't believers – don't rush it; take baby steps. Set small, easily reachable goals at the beginning to let them see they can achieve success.

Children who feel academically lost and discouraged need someone to take a special interest in them. The initial discussions you had to uncover their real feelings have to be followed up by setting regular time aside for them. If you do this, they will start to feel that there is a light at the end of the tunnel (even though they may balk at your pushing them, because at this stage they are still not convinced).

Many teachers have talked about how they had to experiment to find just the right way to teach a particular concept to a child. Tackling their learning problem from different angles can lead to surprising successes. An outgoing, extroverted child, for example, may find it intolerable to sit for long periods in order to memorize multiplication tables. What would work better is to place them in a study group with friends where the social aspect provides more motivation for learning. Consider whether your student is a visual or auditory learner. Some children even learn best through movement.

Tips for helping students progress:

- ✎ Create a warm, safe and supportive atmosphere in your classroom.
- ✎ Don't play favorites. Give attention to each student.
- ✎ Let them know that you respect the things they are interested in.
- ✎ Greet them warmly when they return to class from an absence.

- Don't make negative comments on or about their work, instead, focus on what they are doing well and build on that. Remember, positive comments will improve performance just as negative comments will lower it.
- Let them feel free to make mistakes.
- Set goals you know they can reach.
- Chart their success.
- Tap into peer support to help struggling students.
- Suggest to the student's parents that they hire a very encouraging tutor.

Another idea is to pair someone who has a particular strength with someone who has not enjoyed a subject and/or has done poorly in it. Their job is twofold: to motivate that person so they enjoy the subject, and to help them become good at it. This could be a four-month project, after which evaluations are taken to see what progress was made.

The possible benefits:

- There is nothing more satisfying than teaching. It means you have learned something well and savored the joy of helping someone else learn it.
- When we teach others, we integrate the knowledge better, and may even expand our own knowledge base of the subject.
- It develops a social interest and empathy in students so that they care about others.
- It establishes closer friendships in the class.
- It helps find ways to overcome negative attitudes and poor performance.
- It helps students realize that anyone can overcome difficulty in a subject.

## Dealing with the problem in the class meeting

Having the teacher say "you can do it" is important, but what will have the biggest impact is having the child's peers say it.

That's because they know that the class won't say it just to make them feel better (as a teacher might), they have to really feel it. Discussions about this kind of problem at a class meeting can be very beneficial. Unless the child specifically requests that you bring it up at a meeting, don't bring up their problem. Instead, speak in generalities. A good way to start is with an open-ended question that will help the class reflect on these kinds of learning obstructions. "Why do you think someone would have trouble with a subject?" Most children will answer that it's because the person is not very smart. Your job here is to prove that this is not true. Ask if they have ever known someone who was doing very well in one subject but not in another? If so, you can then conclude that it's not a case of intelligence. Then you can ask them to explore possible reasons why people do well. It might be that:

- they have confidence in themselves
- they have a deep interest in the subject
- they work hard

Use good opened-ended questions like the above to have the class come up with the realization that people do poorly for exactly the opposite reason that they do well:

- they don't have confidence in themselves
- they don't care about the subject
- they don't work hard

Once you have established how and why people do well or not well, you are ready to enlist the enthusiasm and social interest of the class. Statements like "We can do well at the difficult subjects with each other's help" will be of benefit.

Then ask the class: "What are some ways that we can help someone who is having difficulty with a subject?"

Here are some ideas that other classes have come up with:

- Peer tutoring (you could take a sociometric survey – see chapter 15 – and find out which students would be willing to teach and be taught by others).

✎ Group study (rote learning is often boring and therefore more effective in social groups).

✎ Have a homework assignment bin that the teacher keeps filled with work sheets.

✎ The class can help each other set and track goals. ("By the end of next week you will know all the kings and queens of England.")

✎ The teacher can set aside time during the day for group work.

✎ Make progress charts so they can see how much they are learning.

Occasionally you will find a child so open that she will allow you to bring her academic problem up at a class meeting (provided you have an empathetic group). This is good because you can now use the power of the peer group to help solve her problem. The format is identical to the general discussion, the difference being that the class is talking about her specifically. For example, if she says she isn't smart enough to get it, call for a show of hands to see how many students think she is smart enough. Our experience is that most children are easier on each other than themselves. Therefore, you will now have most or all of the class telling her she can do it, which is a powerful message indeed.

## Reporting to parents

Teachers would do well to remind themselves about the intense sensitivity that parents feel when receiving a report on their child. For many parents, a child's performance is a direct reflection of their own parenting skills. A lot of teachers discourage parents by telling them of their child's shortcomings in the classroom, and the parents, in turn, pass on the discouragement to the child. It can be very distressing to hear a lot of negatives about your child, especially if it's phrased as a label. As a general rule, negative labels (lazy, problem child, immature, slow, etc.,) are counterproductive. Some teachers make pronouncements that lock the child into a certain level, such as "your child is not an A student." Often, they are wrong. You've probably heard the story about Albert Einstein, whose parents were told that he would never be good at math. Parents are so sensitive to negative comments that we have often seen them break down in tears when serious problems are brought up. If a parent leaves with a feeling of failure or discouragement, it's hard for them to give the child the encouragement, support, and hope they need to pull themselves out of their problems.

All discussions with parents about the problems their children are having should be phrased as simply and objectively as possible. One good rule of thumb is to always try and sandwich negative comments between two positive ones. Another is to never bring up a problem without including a strategy that outlines what you intend to do about it. A third is to always include the parents in the problem solving process. A fourth is to try and imagine what you would feel like if you were the parent sitting across from you, as in the scenario that follows:

*Lena is the mother of an eight-year-old boy who has had ongoing problems at school. She's concerned, but not too sure about what she should do about it. After years of having to sit in parent-teacher meetings and listening to long lists of her son's shortcomings, she has come to dread the process. After a particularly bad report card, Lena attends another meeting. She can guess what's coming.*

*Teacher:* "Andrew's work is still falling far below the school board's requirements, I'm afraid. He still refuses to listen when I give the class instruction, so he rarely knows what we're working on. And, his behavior is disturbing others in the class. He just doesn't seem to know how to buckle down and get at it. Nothing I try seems to work. Quite frankly, I've almost given up hope that he will complete his year."

Without a positive plan that moves toward a solution, Lena leaves the meeting devastated and full of negative feelings. She's angry with Andrew for his failures, and also disappointed with the teacher for being so negative and hopeless about her child, who she dearly loves. In this angry state, she confronts Andrew when she gets home, which leads to a huge argument that solves nothing but leaves the two of them upset and nowhere near a solution. The next day, Andrew shows up at school even less inclined to work. The "hopelessness" of his situation that was communicated to his mother has been communicated to him.

This meeting would have been much more helpful for everyone concerned if the teacher had pointed out some areas Andrew had improved in or was enthusiastic about. She should have also come up with a plan of attack, with provisions to meet again with Lena to check on progress. Teachers can also use these meetings to educate parents about the goals of misbehavior. For that purpose, use the idea of the goals (chapter 5) to help explain the child's behavior to the parents. Here is how the meeting could have gone better:

*Teacher:* "*I'm pleased that Andrew is so quick to offer help when it is needed. This shows that his strength is his compassion for others However, I can also see that Andrew is misbehaving at times in order to get attention. To handle this, I plan to ignore his misbehavior when possible and give him attention when he does act appropriately. As for his work, he is behind in both math and language arts. However, I will be willing to spend extra time with him so he can catch up in these areas, and maybe even give him some extra homework. I am confident we'll see substantial improvement if we work together on this. I have noticed that Andrew responds well to extra help. If you have any ideas or insights about how to help him, I would like to talk about it.*"

In general, it will help make your job easier (and prove most beneficial to the child) if you help parents increase their parenting skill level. This isn't always easy because resources for parents are scarce. It would be useful, therefore, if you could help set up parenting courses at your school or school district so the parents of your students could learn useful strategies in a supportive atmosphere.

# CHAPTER 13

# Problem solving & conflict resolution

You are an adult. You've been around the block a few times, and because of your experience, you can see a problem developing and quickly figure out how to come up with different ways of dealing with it. You might not realize it, but problem solving is a skill that has to be learned and practiced. Life is always throwing complications our way. You might say that a truly successful person is one who is good at solving these problems. Our fascination with movies, plays, and literature is in many ways due to our interest in stories about people who have overcome problems.

Our goal as caregivers should be to develop this ability in our children so they can feel confident in handling life's problems. A child who is given responsibility from an early age and asked to participate in problem solving and decision making, is going to be better at doing this as an adult as well as while they are children. One of the fallacies embedded in our autocratic past is that teaching obedience is the same as teaching problem solving. When you are asked to be obedient your mind is in neutral. You don't think, you just do or not do. You are passively carrying out someone else's will.

*John is a grade two student whose class job is to feed the goldfish every morning. His teacher has shown him exactly how to do this, and has emphasized that just the right amount of food must be given to the fish. To make sure he doesn't put in too much, the teacher measures out the correct amount for him every day, so all he has to do is put it in the fish tank. John also knows his teacher wants him to return to his seat and be sitting there when the bell rings to start the day's class. One morning, John's teacher is sick and a supply teacher is sent in to take his place. The supply teacher doesn't know about the fish-feeding routine and doesn't leave any food for John to give to the fish. John goes to the tank and is puzzled to find no food there. He doesn't know what to do about it and is trying to think when the bell rings. Realizing he is now "out of position," John runs to his seat and is sitting there like a good boy when the supply teacher begins the lesson. Everything is running smoothly, except that the fish are swimming around hungry. The next morning, John brings up the problem with the fish to the supply teacher who, a little harassed with her new class, tells John to just feed them, but cautions him not to give them too much. Now John is worried. He has never measured the food before and he's worried about giving them too much. As he stands there worrying, it becomes easier for him to just not feed the fish. He's been so used to someone doing it for him that he doesn't have the skill or the confidence to figure out how to do it himself. Besides, it's time for the bell to ring again. John goes and sits in his seat and the fish go hungry for a second day. If the teacher doesn't come back soon, the class's fish are in real trouble.*

John was not encouraged to do problem solving on his own, or to develop his judgment. The job in no way challenged him to grow or to learn. He had learned how to be obedient, but not how to adapt to a changing situation.

John's teacher should have taken a small risk with the fish and let him do the whole feeding routine on his own. He would not only have learned how to measure the correct amount of food, but he would have also gotten used to being in charge of it himself, instead of expecting the adults to make his decisions for him.

Teachers and parents often make this mistake. It's an easy one to make and quite understandable. The curriculum has to be taught. In the effort to maintain order in a classroom of 30 kids, who are bursting with exuberant energy and aching to be outside, is it any wonder we just want everyone to sit down and do as they're told? The challenge, however, is to not only teach the three R's, but also the skills to navigate through and overcome the constant swirl of problems and obstacles that life throws at us. The way it has been in the past, learning the one often meant not learning the other. That is one of the reasons why harnessing the power of the group is so important – when you make the problem of maintaining discipline in the classroom everyone's problem, you not only solve it, you teach the class how to solve other problems in their lives. And, as your students see problems being solved in constructive and cooperative ways, they come to realize – to really believe – that problems can be solved that way.

The ability to solve problems in a creative, constructive way is an invaluable life skill that all too few people have. Knowing how to solve problems, especially interpersonal ones, helps people deal effectively with the most important elements in their lives, such as their work or marriage.

## The nuts and bolts of problem solving

People who are confident, with high levels of self-esteem, overcome problems better than others because they have other attributes, such as flexibility, perseverance, the ability to work hard, open mindedness and optimism. Here are the tools needed for good problem solving:

✎ Prediction. This is the ability to look into the future and see the consequences of our actions, decisions, or choices. As we have said, children tend to live in the present, so they have to be helped with this skill. You teach it by asking the right kinds of questions – "What will happen if you don't study for your test?" "What will happen if you invite the new girl at school over to your house for playtime?" You also teach it by allowing children to experience the consequences of their actions. A pampered child who is sheltered from unpleasant consequences doesn't learn how to look forward. If he forgets his mittens and his mother brings them to school, he never learns to keep them where he can find them and to wear them on cold days so his hands won't get cold. He never learns why it's important to be organized and prepared.

✎ Creativity. Creative people don't box themselves into only one way of doing things. They can come up with all kinds of ways to solve a problem. They are flexible and fluid. If one solution doesn't pan out, they are comfortable with trying others. You can stimulate this in your students by asking questions like: "That didn't work, so what would be another way to tackle the problem?"

✎ Self-esteem. This is a part of problem solving because people who have confidence in their judgment and ability can believe in their decisions. If you don't think what you are doing will work, you may be setting yourself up for a self-fulfilling prophesy.

✎ Optimism. Seeing the positive in people, in yourself, and in life in general makes you a better problem solver. Pessimists don't try much because they don't think anything is a good idea.

✎ Research. The ability to seek out and use resources, whether it's the Internet, the library, friends, or experts, is one of the most valuable tools for solving problems. Information is power, and you have to teach your students how to access it. If they don't know an answer, telling them how to find it is infinitely better than giving it to them.

✎ Realistic private logic. Private logic is our own personal group of beliefs about ourselves, others, and the world. Let's say your private logic says that no one can be trusted. That, of course, is not true, but having this as your private logic will greatly hinder your problem-solving abilities.

For instance, you wouldn't be able to ask anyone for advice because you wouldn't trust them. The converse – that everyone is trustworthy and you can believe what anyone says – can also hinder problem solving. Having a realistic private logic that many but not necessarily all people can be trusted, goes a long way toward effective problem solving.

✎ Empathy. In order to solve a problem that involves another person, you must be able to put yourself in the other person's shoes to see how the problem affects them. Understanding a problem from someone else's perspective is an important part of problem solving and it must be learned. It's important to plant this seed early – the idea that other people have a point of view, and that the best way to solve a problem is to listen to one another, to respect others' opinions, and to incorporate these opinions into solutions. One excellent way to cultivate empathy is to give children an opportunity to act out problems in front of the class. This is called role playing.

## Role Playing

Role playing consists of actually acting out a little scenario in front of the class that depicts the essential aspects of a problem that a student is having, or that two or more students are having with one another. This method is used when discussing the problem has not turned out to be helpful. For example, sometimes young or shy children, children from different cultures, or children who have suffered emotional trauma, may not be able to express themselves well. These children may benefit from role playing, because they can act out their feelings better than they can verbalize them. Acting out the problem allows them to visualize it, to analyze their feelings and the feelings of others, and to then find a solution.

When a child plays a role, he enters into the world of another person. This is a growth experience because it helps him feel and understand the emotions of others. It is excellent training in the development of empathy and compassion for others. It also gives the child a chance to hear other points of view. The wonderful thing about this experience is that they learn in an atmosphere of safety – it's not a real situation, so they can experiment more without having to take psychological risks.

Role playing also lays bare the motivations behind various misbehaviors. If a child acts out the part of a bully, she then has insight into how a bully feels and why he might be doing it, while the bully who is watching can also have insight into his own actions.

## Problems that can be played out

Young children:

- dealing with older kids in the playground
- older siblings at home
- threatening animals
- problems with adults
- making friends
- inviting someone to play
- confronting someone with an "I" message

Children aged 6-12:

- misbehavior in class
- being bullied
- being teased
- being excluded
- being ganged up on
- being called names

Teens:

- being excluded from a clique
- being ostracized
- being belittled
- saying "no" to unacceptable requests

✎ dating
✎ dealing with intimate relationships
✎ difficulties with the teacher
✎ gang-related problems
✎ interruptions in class

## The ten steps of role playing

1. Talk about the problem you are going to be role playing.
2. Make sure the class really wants to act out the situation, otherwise it will be hard to find volunteers.
3. Choose the participants, preferably those who have volunteered. Avoid choosing students that were volunteered or nominated by others.
4. Start immediately. Don't talk too much about the situation or the group will lose spontaneity.
5. Make sure each person knows the role he is to play. Name tags for the role such as "brother" "teacher" etc., are helpful. Props help but are not necessary because students easily jump into their roles.
6. Prepare the class for what to observe and how to look for it (the behavior, the goals, and the motivation). First let the participants act out the problem, then let the class analyze the solution verbally. Lastly, let the participants act out the solution.
7. Give encouragement and assistance only when needed, otherwise let them be spontaneous. Don't let it go too long.
8. As soon as the problem is clear, stop the action. Have the participants stay where they are so that people can clearly visualize the problem.
9. Discuss the feelings of each participant in the play. The observers can then make their comments and evaluations. How did it start? What was the misunderstanding? Which role was responsible for the problem? What could have been done? What should be done now? What was the purpose of the behavior of the person causing the problem?

10. Using the same or different actors, reenact the scene again, but this time with a solution or even many different solutions. Get the feelings of the actors and the group as to whether the solutions will work. Encourage everyone to try new ideas. Ask them to report about the problem at the next class meeting.

### Role playing nuts and bolts

The role-playing cast should be selected by the teacher to avoid students volunteering others in order to humiliate them. Cast against type. For example, don't cast the bully in the bully role. Select the main character first so that the others can see how the role they volunteer for relates to the main character. Make the selections quickly so that the action can start immediately.

Role playing is fun, but the teacher has to make an effort to keep the class on track and their sights on the problem enacted. If anyone is acting inappropriately or silly, remove the child and find another actor. The child can be returned for the solution if he is ready to participate seriously. Of course, children will laugh at certain funny situations being enacted.

There are two acts to our role playing. The first act is always about the problem, the second, about the solution, or the many different solutions, to that problem. As soon as the problem is clearly stated and understood through the play, the teacher can stop the action. (This can take less than a minute but should not be more than a few minutes long.) Talk about possible reasons why the problem happened and then discuss various solutions. Then, reenact the problem with different solutions.

# Conflict Resolution

Problem solving is important because life, like good drama, is full of conflict. We can, to a certain degree, reduce the conflict in our lives, but no one can eliminate it. We all have different goals and needs and they are constantly at odds with each other.

Someone's need to mow the lawn, for example, interferes with someone else's need to sleep in on a Saturday morning. We not only have to be good at resolving conflicts ourselves, but we have to teach our students how to do so as well. The following is a tried and true method of conflict resolution developed by famed educator John Dewey that has been used in countless schools and counseling sessions. It can be used in a class meeting or on its own, especially when you have exhausted all other forms of solving a particular problem, or when people are very upset.

## The six-step problem-solving method

*Step One – Defining the problem.*

State your problem:

✎ Don't make a demand or emphasize your wants. Instead, state the problem simply and clearly with as few words as possible. For example: "The class is generating too much noise and no one can work." "I am aware that there is bullying going on." "I have observed that there is a lot of fighting going on at lunch time."

*Step Two – Cooperative brainstorming*
*to find possible solutions*

Each person (the teacher, the students involved, or even the whole class) offers various solutions to the problem. No evaluation of these solutions are discussed at this stage. All possible solutions are written down. You can even encourage outrageous solutions ("We can have naps after lunch so we will be in better moods") because not only will it prove to be fun, it will also help students be more creative.

*Step Three – Evaluating the creative solutions*

This is the part that determines which solutions students like, and which they want to exclude. You can do this by asking them to raise their hand if they don't like a solution. Cross off the list any solution that they feel will not work. The solutions that are left can be expanded and clarified to reach a final decision by consensus.

### Step Four – Clarify and restate decisions

The teacher should turn to the student who originally made the suggestion that remains on the list and ask them to explain what they had in mind. After the explanation, ask the rest of the class, "Is that the way everyone understands it and will this still be acceptable to you all?" At this point you are making sure they understand fully and are in agreement.

### Step Five – Agreeing how to carry out the decision

Talk about what will be done. Who will do it? When should it be done? Where will it take place? How will it get done?

### Step Six – Evaluating the success of the solutions

Agree upon a time to discuss the results. Ideally, this would be at the next class meeting. Ask the class the following questions:

✎ Has the problem been dealt with effectively?
✎ Are you satisfied with the results?

If the solution didn't work, go through the conflict resolution procedure again. When solutions don't work, it is important to emphasize that this is not an indication of failure. People learn a great deal even when things don't work.

## When conflict resolution doesn't work

Some teachers report that they are very uncomfortable with the process of conflict resolution in the classroom. They fear losing control of the class if they allow the students to come up with solutions to conflicts. And, let's face it, many adults can't quite bring themselves to believe that children are able to come up with helpful solutions, or that they have the wit or the experience to be able to tell right from wrong.

Let's look at this fear of giving up your position of power and authority – of not doing what you were hired to do, which is to be the leader and decision maker of the class. This is an understandable concern. And, even deeper down, there is the worry that the students will come up with a solution you are dead set against.

The answer is to remind yourself that you are working with the idea of consensus. That doesn't mean it's a compromise – a compromise is a solution that both parties are only partially happy with. What conflict resolution strives for is a solution that both parties can fully accept. But it also means that if even one person says no, the idea is dead. Everyone has a veto including the teacher. You can, and should, exercise this veto when you feel you are right. Here's an example:

*Seven-year-old Becky has been given the job of collecting money for the milk program. Feeling drunk with power, Becky refuses to order milk for a student who doesn't have the right change. Using the six-step conflict resolution system, the class decided that her job should be given to someone else. The teacher, knowing that having this job was important to Becky's self-esteem, and also realizing that it was unlikely that the problem would happen again, voted against her losing the job. Becky, who promised not to do it again, also voted against it.*

Another thing to consider is that it's possible for the teacher to be wrong, and sometimes a lone dissenter can turn out to be right. It should also be remembered that decisions can be reversed. Nothing is written in stone here, in fact, they are written in chalk. Things can be changed and changed without anyone losing face, and most decisions can be reversed without serious consequences. It's good for children to learn to be flexible, to be willing to say: "I made a decision that was not the best decision. Now it's time to try something else." Have the courage to say: "We tried a solution last week that didn't really work because Rocco still feels he is left out at playtime. So let's look at the problem again and see if we can find a better solution."

Including the class in solving problems that crop up over the year may feel uncomfortable for someone who is used to solving these problems themselves. But in return, you are losing some of the stress that comes from the feeling that you must be in total control. As you develop the skill of using problem solving techniques with your students, your level of discomfort will evaporate. We have heard people say that it is very liberating not to feel that you have to be the one to solve every single problem that comes up. And it can be very empowering for the students, who are not used to having a say in the decisions that affect their lives at school.

Finally, always remember to look at the positive side, and stress to your students that:

- ✎ It was a democratic process that included everyone's ideas.
- ✎ The group worked together cooperatively.
- ✎ They are all getting better at conflict resolution through practice.
- ✎ The people involved formed a closer relationship.
- ✎ They developed the courage to be imperfect, and learned that it is alright to make mistakes.
- ✎ They have shown that they can contribute to the solution of class problems.

# CHAPTER 14

# Communications skills: how to talk, how to listen

Learning how to communicate in a respectful manner is critical for anyone wanting to have a positive relationship with a child. One crucial aspect of showing that respect is listening to them and taking what they say seriously. This lets them know that we care about them. A good listener conveys a feeling of empathy. They actually seem to be interested in what you are saying.

When talking to children, talk with the same amount of respect you would give to one of your friends. This means accepting their right to have their own feelings or opinions, even though you may not necessarily agree with them. Good communication helps people form healthy relationships by doing everything from solving problems and developing empathy, to learning about and accepting the world and themselves.

Many of us have had the frustrating experience of trying to explain something important to a person who just wasn't getting it. It is often the case in such situations, that one or both of the individuals is communicating poorly (see the sidebar on roadblocks to communication).

# THE ROADBLOCKS TO COMMUNICATION

Just because you're having a conversation doesn't necessarily mean you're communicating well. For instance, we have all experienced these common obstacles:

▼ monologues

▼ demands

▼ orders and commands

▼ warnings

▼ advising

▼ lecturing

▼ criticizing

▼ blaming

▼ ridiculing

▼ directing

▼ threatening

▼ moralizing

*(Source: Thomas Gordon, Teacher Effectiveness Training)*

Here are two examples of a typical teacher-student exchange, the first being relatively ineffective and the second working to everyone's benefit.

*Morgan is a first grader. When it's time to go outside for recess, he's always the last one out the door. In fact, it sometimes takes him so long to get his winter clothes on that he misses most of the play period. The teacher ends up spending a lot of time directing him and trying to get him ready. A typical Morgan lament is:*

*Morgan: "I've got too many clothes to put on. It's too hard. I need you to help me."*

*Teacher (in an angry, impatient tone): "You're just not trying hard enough, Morgan. You're a big boy now. All the other children managed to put their clothes on and are outside – you're the only one left. If you don't get yourself ready in one minute, you'll have to spend recess at the office. I can't take any more time with you on this."*

In this example, there are numerous roadblocks to effective communication, including lecturing, blaming, criticizing, and warning. The teacher's angry response succeeded in quickly shutting down the communication process. The solution presented, which was for Morgan to dress faster, was a one-sided solution, rather than the two-way dialogue it should have been. This is a very common way teachers and parents have of talking to children – they give the solution and then berate the child for not coming up with it themselves, or else they attach blame. Here is another way to handle it without causing the frustration and discouragement that results from poor communication.

*Morgan: "I've got too many clothes to put on. It's too hard. I need you to help me."*

*Teacher: "You sound as if you feel you can't handle this."*

*Morgan: "Yeah. That's why I want you to help me."*

*Teacher:* "So you don't think you can get your snow suit on without my help.

*Morgan:* "That's right. There's too many clothes. I hate winter. Why can't I stay inside?"

*Teacher:* "You find getting ready so hard you would rather miss recess?"

*Morgan:* "Right."

*Teacher:* "Since we have a school rule that says all children have to be outside for recess, we'll have to figure out a way to help you get dressed. Could you think of something that might help you get dressed faster?"

*Morgan:* "All the boys I like to play with go out first. Maybe they could wait for me?"

*Teacher:* "You think it would help if Mike and Daniel waited for you?"

*Morgan:* "Yeah."

*Teacher:* "Would you be willing to talk to them about that after recess today?"

*Morgan:* "I guess so."

*Teacher:* "Alright. Let me know what you and the other two boys decide."

Morgan now goes about putting his clothes on without too much trouble while the teacher does her own work.

Instead of just giving Morgan the solution to the problem, his teacher used active listening while refusing to provide undue service. This allowed Morgan to explain what the real problem was (which she would not have been able to divine), and come up with his own solution. The fact that Morgan proceeded to get dressed independently indicates that he felt encouraged by this conversation. (Remember at the beginning how incompetent he felt?) Morgan's problem – and it is his problem – was typical of the myriad of problems everyone faces throughout their day. By allowing him to solve the problem himself, Morgan's teacher also allowed him to begin to use his reason and judgment. Whether or not he came up with the best solution is not important. The important thing is that he has had an opportunity to test his own solution to one of life's problems. If his teacher had handed him the solution on a plate, even though it would probably have saved her a few minutes of her time, she would have denied him a chance to hone this valuable life skill. A golden rule of the classroom should be to never offer a child a solution she could come up with herself. Put another way, never think for a child, because when you do, you prevent them from learning how to think for themselves.

## The results of poor communication

Most of us assume that any kind of communication is good, but ineffective or negative kinds of communication, such as put-downs, sarcasm, and comparisons, can be harmful, especially to young minds that are developing new attitudes about themselves and the world around them. In fact, poor communication and negative messages can result in all kinds of problems, including low self-esteem and poor problem-solving skills, as well as many of the neurotic defenses with which people arm themselves.

There are lots of obstacles to good communication that hinder the free exchange of ideas and feelings. Many of them are holdovers from authoritarian times when the goal of most communication, certainly where children were involved, was to enforce compliance, often through fear.

Here are some classic examples of poor communication:

✎ Giving orders. The message here is that your will is all-important and what the child wants means very little. ("Put that ball down and take this to the office for me immediately.") Orders don't allow children to develop problem-solving skills or learn how to think independently. They can result in anger, resistance, and hostility.

✎ Threatening. Usually following a direct order. ("If you don't shape up immediately, you're going to fail grade six.") This can cause children to feel frightened. Although it may force them to submit, it can also result in the child becoming more stubborn and even calling your bluff to see if you will follow through.

✎ Criticizing and ridiculing. ("That was a pretty sloppy presentation. Did you leave your brain in the closet this morning?") This is the best way to lower self-esteem, especially when it comes from someone as looked-up-to as a teacher. Negative statements can easily become self-fulfilling prophecies. The person who is told she is inconsiderate enough times may well end up believing that is what and who she is. A person labeled as mean will have their meanness reinforced.

✎ Being condescending. ("Here, let me do that, you're a little bit too young [or small] to manage it.") Condescension presents the child with a diminished image of herself and a superior image of the teacher. It's a subtle but nonetheless powerful put-down that emphasizes the child's weakness. This can make the child feel ineffective and small, which also lowers self-esteem.

✎ Providing ready-made solutions. ("You two play with the ball at the morning recess and the other two can use it this afternoon.") This is the "teacher knows best" approach. It's hard for us to refrain from solving what to us are simple problems. But even when it works, you rob your students of the experience of solving their own problems. It not only subtly conveys the idea that you don't think they can find a solution, it also habituates them looking to authority figures to do their thinking for them. This approach is particularly resented by teenagers and children that are seeking the goal of power.

✎ Praise. Often confused with encouragement. ("Has everyone seen Cathy's test results? You are a first-rate math student, Cathy.") It's hard to believe that something as positive as praise can stand in the way of good communication, but it does. This is so because praise, when used to influence or motivate the child to act in some way you consider desirable, will often be seen by the child for just what it is, a form of manipulation. Even worse, when a child is feeling bad or unhappy about herself, praise can actually reinforce her negative feelings and hurt the teacher-child relationship because you can be seen as not knowing the child at all – "the real me." In the classroom, praise can also be seen as a negative evaluation by those who have not been praised.

The hallmarks of good communication include:

✎ Listening in an empathetic, nonjudgmental way.
✎ Keeping your voice friendly and your mind open.
✎ Allowing for disagreements.
✎ Being respectful.

## The results of good communication

✎ The student walks away believing his feelings have been understood.
✎ The student hasn't felt pressured to buy into someone else's solution.
✎ It enhances the relationship so that there is greater cooperation in problem solving.
✎ One person feels closer to another and feels they can share almost anything with them.
✎ A respectful tone can raise someone's self-esteem.

Imagine for a moment that you are a child that is constantly exposed to poor communication methods. The following are ways that children could be expected to respond:

✎ Merely say what the authority figure expects you to say.

✎ Avoid expressing your feelings.

✎ Always ask for permission.

✎ Do not express your thoughts.

✎ Keep your wants and needs to yourself.

✎ Play stupid.

✎ Do not question or disagree.

✎ Act as if everything is OK.

People who practice effective communication skills avoid these discouraged responses.

And remember, to truly have open communication you must allow for disagreements – for the statement of both positive and negative feelings – without fear. One of the most important concepts for good communication is that of social equality. In our relationships (with the exception of friendships), we have been raised to relate to people as either being above or below us. This makes it difficult to communicate with people we consider to be either in authority or subordinate to us. As a result, communicating with people on a mutually respectful level requires skills most of us don't have. Is it any wonder then that there are serious problems in marriages, and in the relationships between parents and children, as well as between teachers and students? If we are going to learn to communicate more effectively, what better place is there to start than in our own classrooms?

## Focus on Feelings

At the centre of good communication with children is the understanding of their emotional selves, of their feelings. Try to imagine the problem from the other person's point of view. This doesn't have anything to do with logically solving a problem, which is often our first and only thought – although solutions will logically flow from good communication. What good communication is about is accepting the feelings of others without judgment. This is even more important, albeit more difficult, when dealing with negative emotions.

*Martha's teacher insists that anyone getting below a B grade must have the test signed by their parents. Martha, who has been struggling to maintain a C average, has been putting less and less effort into her work. She is confronted by her teacher after a particularly bad test result.*

*Teacher: "Martha, I can see that you were working so much harder at the beginning of the year. Can you tell me what happened?"*

*Martha: "What difference does it make? I never get more than a C+, so I always have to get my test signed anyway. My parents always get mad at me. I'm in trouble when I get a C or less."*

*Teacher: "It sounds like you're giving up, and you're angry because you are getting into trouble with your parents because of the rule about getting tests signed."*

*Martha: "You got it."*

If you hit the feeling right on, you will get an agreement from the child. If you get it wrong, they'll tell you. You have, in fact, proven that you really see what they are going through. When a person feels understood, many positive things happen. There is a diminishing of stress as they recognize that what they are going through is not a unique situation. They feel connected. They feel they're okay. What you have done by listening and understanding is to lay the groundwork that will allow you to work with them in the future to solve problems. At that moment of understanding, you become an empathetic ally to whom they can turn to in times of stress.

When you are not using good communication techniques, it's easy to invalidate children's feelings. Here are some examples:

*Student: "This is stupid. I'll never learn math."*
*Teacher: "Not if you don't buckle down and start working harder."*

*Student: "It's always the popular kids who get chosen for the lead roles in the play."*
*Teacher: "That's not true. You have as much chance as anyone."*

*Student:* "My partner didn't do any of the work. It's not fair that I had to share an 'A' with him."
*Teacher:* "It's up to you to make sure the work is done equally."

Those reactions may be accurate and true, but they brush aside the child's point of view. You are wrong, we are saying, so you shouldn't be feeling that way. You have invalidated their emotions. Just because you are "logically" right doesn't mean you are "psychologically" right. The starting point for having any influence on students, or developing problem-solving abilities with them, starts with understanding and accepting their feelings.

In order to get it right, you have to put yourself in the other person's shoes. Imagine what it would be like for you to be overwhelmed by a difficult subject. Try and understand all of the frustration you would experience, the fear of angry parents, and the ridiculing by your peers that you would undergo. If you are truly able to imagine the other person's perspective, it won't come out sounding artificial or false when you say things like, "So you're really feeling totally lost when it comes to math these days?" Or, "You're disappointed in not being picked for one of the leads, and you think the selection process was unfair." Or, "You see yourself being used by Bobby, and you are upset with a system that lets someone get the same mark as you when they didn't do much of the work."

Negative emotions are hard to deal with. Some of the common negative emotions that we often try and gloss over are: jealousy, fear, dislike, hopelessness, and anger. We either try to ignore them or tell our students that they shouldn't feel that way.

As an exercise, take the following three statements and try to answer them in a way that validates their emotions.

- ✎ "My best friend has been ignoring me all week."
- ✎ "The music teacher gave me a "D" and my friend got a "B", but I practiced more."
- ✎ "I'm so fat! I hate myself!"

# Effective communication skills

The following are the skills that need to be practiced by teachers in order to become effective communicators:

## Listening

The first step to good communication is listening. Sometimes adults are better at talking then listening. That's because communication is often thought of as a "talking" skill, but a large part of good communication is listening. Effective listening requires both verbal and nonverbal skills. The idea is to try and understand what the other person is going through by being empathetic, to make sure we understand the content of what they are saying, as well as what they are feeling. To be a good listener, one has to remain silent while the other person is talking and maintain good eye contact.

## Good listening skills

Being a good listener is one of the most unappreciated of the social skills. The benefits of good listening skills in the classroom are:

- Helps children label their emotions and understand themselves better.
- Children are more willing to talk.
- Helps children defuse strong negative feelings.
- Children feel you care about them.
- It's a form of encouragement and therefore raises self-esteem.
- It demonstrates unconditional acceptance.
- It clarifies who the problem belongs to.
- It models good listening skills for the child.

The requirements for good listening skills:

- A deep sense of trust in your students' ability to solve their own problems.

✎ An acceptance of their feelings, even negative ones.

✎ A strong desire to help them with their problems.

✎ The ability to respect the confidentiality of their conversations.

## The two kinds of listening skills

### 1. Passive listening

As the name suggests, passive listening requires the listener to be in an open and receptive frame of mind. The listener doesn't worry about paraphrasing or reflecting back the feeling or the content of the message (therefore no words are needed). Instead, they rely on relaxed, open body language with arms uncrossed.

Don't have any barriers, such as a desk, between you and the child. Maintain good eye contact and allow the child to talk freely. Don't interrupt, but respond only with encouraging sounds and gestures, such as "uh huh" and nodding of the head.

Even though you aren't saying it directly, remaining silent is in itself an indication that you accept what the child is saying. This encourages the child to continue talking. Sometimes just listening is enough. It's harder to do than you might think, because our tendency is often to rush in and give our opinion. Passive listening takes great restraint.

The only problem with passive listening is that the child might not feel fully understood because you are not giving them feedback. If all you get from someone is encouraging nods and sounds, you may wonder if they truly get what you are saying. If you feel the situation requires you to help the student understand their feelings better, or that you should move into problem solving, switch to active listening.

### 2. Active listening (sometimes called "reflective listening")

This involves listening to what the child has just said and paraphrasing the content and feeling back to them. Active listening is a more complete response than passive listening. You are giving feedback to the speaker, which allows you to not only carry on a discussion about their feelings or problems, but also for them to correct any misunderstandings you may have.

It works like this: The sender gives the message, and the receiver, using open body language, repeats it back in a way that focuses on the sender's feelings and pertinent details. The receiver doesn't add any of their own ideas, feelings, or suggestions.

Use active listening when the child is upset, tearful, agitated, happy, excited, or confused, or anytime they show signs of strong emotion. It also helps if the child is having difficulty giving a label to what they are feeling.

*Lisa, who is 12, has been skipping swimming class. After missing three classes, her teacher calls her in for a talk about the problem. He avoids probing with questions about why she isn't swimming, but instead asks open-ended questions.*

*Teacher:* "Can we talk about why you've missed so many swim classes?"

*Lisa:* (looking worried and at every part of the room but at him) "I don't know. I've been busy. I haven't felt like it."

*Teacher:* (nodding his head in an understanding way) "Uh Huh…"

*The silence and his open, friendly statement encourages Lisa to open up a little.*

*Lisa:* "I'm sorry I've missed so many classes but I don't think I want to go to swimming anymore. The coach is always telling the really good swimmers how great they are but he never says anything nice to me. I think he only likes the good swimmers. I'm thinking of switching to volleyball."

*Teacher:* "How do you know he only likes the good swimmers? "

*Lisa:* "Because he is always with them but he ignores me."

*Teacher:* "It sounds like you have been missing classes because you don't think you're doing as well as the other kids and therefore the coach doesn't like you as much as the others."

*Lisa:* "I just think I would be better at volleyball."

*Teacher:* "So you think if you switched to volleyball you would be more liked? What do you enjoy about swimming anyway?"

*Lisa:* "I like a lot of the kids on the team. I like being in the water and I like trying as hard as I can at something, but I feel embarrassed when I come in last. And I always come in last."

*Teacher:* "So because you are worrying about how well you are doing, you are going to give up something you enjoy?"

*Lisa:* "But I like volleyball too, and I'm better at it."

*Teacher:* "You feel you should only participate in something you're really great at, and only if the coach likes you?"

*Lisa:* "My dad always says if you're going to do something, you should do it well."

*Teacher:* "Uh huh. So your dad is saying, if you're not good at something you should give it up?"

*Lisa:* "No. He didn't say that. He said you should just do things well, but I'm not. So what he really means is that I should try harder."

*Teacher:* "What other reasons are there for taking swimming?"

*Lisa:* "Well, its fun. And I get a lot of exercise. But I still feel like I'm letting everyone down, and that makes the kids not like me so much."

*Teacher:* "Your main worry seems to be that the other kids will be disappointed in your performance and maybe think the less of you and therefore not like you."

*Lisa:* "Yeah. But when you put it that way, it makes me sound like I'm a quitter when things aren't going well. I don't think I like that about myself".

*Teacher:* "Are all the kids finishing in the top of the class?"

*Lisa:* "No. Janine and Daphne don't do so well either."

*Teacher:* "So others aren't doing that well either. Why do you think they're still doing it?"

*Lisa:* "I don't know. Maybe they're just having fun."

*Teacher:* "Do you think any of the other kids would want them to quit because they weren't the best?"

*Lisa:* "No."

*Lisa is quiet and thoughtful for a moment.*

*Teacher:* "What are you thinking about?"

*Lisa:* "I don't know. Maybe I'll start going again."

*Teacher:* "You're thinking about giving it another try. I'm glad you were able to tell me about your worries about swimming. It sounds to me like you are starting to figure out what your real priorities are."

Throughout this dialogue, the teacher attempted to help Lisa identify her mistaken ideas without lecturing or criticizing. The final result of this helpful exchange was to prevent her from running way from a stressful situation.

Active listening can also be used when the child is excited or happy.

*Five-year-old Claire just got a new puppy. At kindergarten, she tells her teacher all about her new pet.*

*Claire:* "She's the cutest little yellow puppy. Her name is Bowser and my parents let her sleep with me."

*Teacher:* "You sound so happy. It must be fun to have a puppy to play with and cuddle up with at night."

*Claire:* "Yes, and I won't be lonely any more. All my friends have brothers and sisters, but I don't. Now I have somebody to play with."

Some active listening phrases are:

- ✎ "What I hear you saying is _____."
- ✎ "It sounds like you are feeling _____."
- ✎ "Let me see if I got that right _____."

Some responses that encourage further dialogue could be:

- ✎ "You're saying _____."
- ✎ "In other words _____."

*Example*

*"I had a hard day at school. I didn't get all my work done and my teacher asked me to stay after school to finish. On top of it all, I feel that my teacher doesn't see how much I have to do – go to basketball practice, and be home in time to finish my homework."*

You can rephrase this statement to include a summation of the content, as well as what you think the feeling is behind what the person is saying.

*"It sounds like you feel overwhelmed with the amount of work and responsibility on your shoulders, and you're also really angry that your teacher doesn't care about how much is on your plate."*

You can paraphrase the content of what a child is saying in your own words by making a brief statement about what the child was experiencing. In order to do this, pay attention to the 5 Ws. For instance, if a student wants to talk about a fight he had during recess, you would ask:

1. Who or what was involved? (the child and his friend)
2. What did they do? (they had a fight)
3. Why did they do it? (because his friend called him a name)
4. When did they do it? (during recess)
5. Where did it happen? (in the schoolyard)

The most important part, however, is to reflect the feeling that the child experienced. Ask yourself, "How would I feel if this happened to me?" After coming up with your own feeling, reflect it back to the child by saying something like: "It sounds like you feel hurt (the emotion) because your friend called you a name (the content)." Paraphrasing also helps you and the child know that you have understood what has been said. Asking questions not only lets you find out more about a situation, but lets the child know you are interested as well. Don't worry if you get it wrong, because the child will correct you.

*Child:* "*I hate Jesse. He took my scooter and didn't give it back until recess.*"

*Teacher:* "*Sounds like you're mad at Jessie for taking your scooter and leaving you with nothing to play with.*"

*Child:* "*No. I'm just mad that he didn't ask me first.*"

*Teacher:* "*Oh, so what made you angry is that Jesse took it without asking.*"

*Child:* "*Right.*"

## Open and closed questions

There are two kinds of questions; open and closed. A closed question looks for specific facts, and only requires a one-word answer, often a yes or a no:

- ✎ "What time did this happen?"
- ✎ "How many people are going with me to the track meet?"
- ✎ "Where were you standing when the fight started?"
- ✎ "Did you finish your homework?"
- ✎ "What game were you playing at recess?"
- ✎ "Who won the baseball game?"
- ✎ "Are you going to buy milk with your lunch today?"

As you can see, closed questions are good for uncovering specific facts to help you make a decision quickly, or even just to gather more information. However, they are not effective when you are trying to deal with emotional situations or conflicts in which you want the child to open up and freely express herself. Closed questions are ineffective when you are trying to encourage dialogue because the child might find this collecting of data irrelevant, or may interpret it as an attempt by the teacher to control the direction of the conversation.

Open-ended questions invite the child to elaborate, without limiting the direction or otherwise controlling the conversation. They also require, or at least open the door to, answers of more than one word:

- ✎ "Why don't you tell me more about that?"
- ✎ "What do you think would happen if…?"
- ✎ "Sounds interesting. How does it work?"
- ✎ "How do you feel about that?"

Sometimes you can help children solve their problems just by asking open-ended questions.

*Student: "I left my project at home. My mom's at work so she can't bring it to me."*

*Teacher: Sounds like you have a tricky problem there. What kind of options can you think of for yourself?"*

*Student: "I can bring it in tomorrow, but I'll lose marks for lateness."*

*Teacher: "That would be a shame, because I know you worked very hard on it. Can you think of any way to get it today?"*

*Student: "I guess I could call my mom and ask her if it's alright for me to walk home at lunch and get it."*

*Teacher: "Sounds like a good plan. Let me know how it works out."*

## The "I" message

An "I" message indicates that you are taking responsibility for your own feelings. A "You" message, on the other hand, attaches blame. "I" messages are effective in resolving problems while

"You" messages lead to power struggles, feelings of guilt, and the lowering of the child's self-esteem. Here are some typical "You" messages: "You are so lazy!" or "You are a real problem here." or "You never help."

These "you" messages attack the child's character.

Here is a typical "I" message: "I feel concerned when you don't eat your lunch because I'm worried you'll be hungry in the afternoon and you won't be able to concentrate."

Notice that there are three distinct parts to an "I" message. One is a statement about how you are feeling ("I feel concerned"). The second is a statement of the problem you are experiencing ("When you don't eat your lunch"). A third is a statement of the consequence of the child's behavior ("You won't be able to concentrate").

The three aspects of the message are: "I feel _____ when you _____ because _____."

Another way of communicating a problem is to state the problem while leaving out the "feeling" aspect, such as: "I can't continue with this lesson while everyone is talking."

## Whose problem is it, anyway?

The important thing to remember is who the problem belongs to. If the problem belongs to the teacher, the teacher must take responsibility for it. It's important to realize that we all interpret events. We give events meaning and we attach an emotion to them. But you must understand that you own that emotion. No one forced you to feel that way. Some people, for example, see humor in the exact same situation where others see pathos. We all filter events through our own emotional screen. It's not the event that causes the emotion, but the ideas, expectations and judgments that we attach to the event.

*Example:* A student is disrespectful to a teacher. The teacher retaliates by saying: "You make me furious!" Even though you would think that most people would react the same way when being called a name, we still have to realize that it is an unconscious decision – a choice we make – when we get upset. But when you use a "You" statement, you are holding someone else responsible for your own emotional state.

Let's take this teacher's dilemma one step further. The verbal abuse by the student gets to the point where it happens every day. The teacher becomes furious every day, and feels totally justified in his fury. After attending a teacher's workshop, this teacher achieves some insight into the goals of this abusive student. He correctly diagnoses the goal of revenge and sets about correcting his response to the provocation. He realizes that to help this student and improve the situation, he can't take the behavior personally. As so often happens when the goal of misbehavior is understood by the teacher, there is a subtle shift in his feelings toward the student, especially when he recognizes his part in the child's goal. He still feels it is hurtful behavior, but he works at changing his knee-jerk reaction to it. He knows the antidote to revengeful behavior is being friendly, initiating inclusive and respectful actions, and taking time to talk to the student. He also avoids punishment but takes every opportunity to show the student that he likes and cares for her. It takes some time, but he realizes that he does in fact have control over how he reacts to and feels about the girl's behavior. We are not saying being angry was the wrong (or right) reaction, but only pointing out how we have more control in how we do react to things than we think. That's why you have to take ownership for your feelings and use "I" messages to show your students that you're doing just that. Think of this the next time you feel like saying: "You make me feel...".

Not convinced? Have you ever been in the heat of an angry argument with someone and the phone rings? You stop arguing, and in your most pleasant, controlled voice, answer the phone. When you hang up, the anger zooms back to the surface and off you go.

Communication processes can also be nonverbal. Our facial expressions and tone of voice communicate more than you might think. For instance, teachers may be condescending or speak as if the children are unable to understand normal conversation. Children are very aware of being talked down to. Always use a respectful tone of voice.

When we criticize children or find fault with what they think, they soon become closed to adults and hide their true thoughts and feelings. We do not always have to tell children their ideas are wrong if we disagree with what they are saying. We have to recognize there are more points of view than our own. Stress that their ideas and viewpoints are important.

Moralizing is another method of creating distance between teachers and children. "I don't want to invite Marty to my party. I don't like him any more." "Oh, you must invite him. You can't not invite someone just because you had a little spat. That would be very rude. We should always make sure we don't leave anyone out. You certainly wouldn't like being the one left out."

Instead of sermons like that, ask the child questions in order to help him and you come up with solutions to problems. For example: "How do you think your friend will feel if you don't invite him to your party?" If you try to solve problems alone, without the children, you lose the opportunity to influence their behavior.

The best way to solve problems is by talking about them and exploring them together. Anger is one of the least admired emotions. That's because it is destructive when it gets out of hand. But anger is also an essential human tool. It is the emotional equivalent of pain; it lets us know something is wrong. Anger is useful in problem solving because it helps us move towards finding a solution. From a teacher's perspective, it lets our students know that what they are doing is unacceptable. The key to anger is to understand what it is and to express it properly.

## Expressing anger

Contrary to popular belief, you are always in control of your anger. Usually, you let yourself become very angry because you want immediate results. Yelling at someone is about power, but you can let a child know that you are angry just by the inflection of your voice, without resorting to screaming. It is all a matter of degree. When you use your anger to intimidate and cause fear, you have gone too far. But on the other hand, you do have to let students know that certain kinds of behavior could result in people becoming angry. The best way to do this is to express your own anger in a firm, serious voice. If someone has broken a window through sheer carelessness, let them know how you feel about it. Tell them why you are angry – that it costs time and money to fix a broken window. (See Problem Solving, chapter 13). When teachers yell all the time, their students can quickly become immune to it ("That's just Ms. Smith screaming again.") But when a teacher or caregiver who seldom yells becomes genuinely angry and expresses it by their tone of voice, the children will pay attention and respond to it. Always remember to state your anger in the form of an "I" statement.

## Communicating in the class meeting

The class meeting is an excellent structure for learning how to listen as well as to speak. It is designed to teach people how to listen to, think about, and incorporate the views of others so that the group can arrive at a solution that, as much as is humanly possible, takes everyone's needs into account.

*Example:* May wants to play soccer at recess but Melina, who owns the soccer ball, says no, there are already too many players and besides, May isn't good enough and will slow the game down. They decide to go to the teacher, known for having the wisdom of Solomon, for arbitration. Both of them have a legitimate point of view but are unable to see the other person's position. If you impose a solution without using proper problem-solving techniques, one of them could feel hurt or angry.

One thing to keep in mind is that the moment the problem is happening may not be the best time to come up with a solution. For one thing, there is not enough time to engage in proper problem solving For another, emotions are running high. The

## Effective communication

Teachers who communicate effectively with their students:

▼ Allow them to express their thoughts and feelings without fear. If every teacher and parent was a good listener – a good communicator – therapists would be out of business.

▼ Let them know you they interested in what they have to say.

▼ Help them feel they are accepted and respected as a person even though you might not agree with them.

▼ Use a respectful tone of voice even when they don't.

▼ Pay full attention to them when they are talking.

▼ Don't interrupt them when they are talking.

▼ Maintain good eye contact.

▼ Don't criticize the child's speech, grammar, or content.

game has been stopped, the schoolyard is alive with its usual noise and chaotic activity, and the clock is ticking down to when the bell will ring. You might want to handle it this way:

*Teacher:* "*I can see this is a problem, but I think we need to talk about it a lot longer than we have time for here on the playground. How would you feel about letting the game continue for now the way it is? We will definitely put it on the agenda so we can talk about it at today's class meeting.*"

Use the meeting to teach the kids how to listen to each other – all of them will learn by watching May and Melina doing it. First ask the two girls if you can use them to show the group how to learn to listen.

Here is an exercise you could try that will help ensure the two parties to this disagreement listen to each other properly and respond to their respective comments (see listening exercises at the end of this chapter). It's important for them to do this, because otherwise they could both just go off on their own tangents without listening at all. (In order to reach the stage where your students are able to use this exercise to solve problems, have them practice this on a made-up story.) Tell them that each girl will have 30 seconds or a minute to give their side of the story. Then the other girl has to repeat it back. To do that, they have to listen intently. Point out to the class that listening is not an easy thing to do and must be learned and practiced. Once both girls have said all they have to say and clearly understood the other's point of view, the entire class joins in to come up with the new rule about playing games at recess. Give them a formal structure to work within. Maybe you could use a chalkboard or flip chart to write down the problem and each of the points both girls make. Here's how it might go:

*Teacher:* "OK May, the idea is that you are going to tell Melina exactly how you feel about the fact that you couldn't play soccer at recess today. To make sure she heard and understood you, Melina will repeat what you said, and then it will be her turn. Alright?"

*May:* "Well, I wanted to play soccer but when I tried to join the game, Melina told me that I couldn't because there were already too many people. But she doesn't own the schoolyard. Who does she think she is?"

*Melina:* "I don't think I own the schoolyard!"

*Teacher:* "You'll have your turn, Melina. But right now it's May's turn. I want you to really listen to what she has to say. May, it's going to be a lot easier for Melina to really listen to you if you don't say anything negative about her. Just tell her what happened and how it made you feel."

*May:* "I wanted to play soccer with everyone else and Melina said *no. It made me feel like there was something wrong with me. Besides, she told me I wasn't good enough to play and that made me mad."*

*Teacher: "Melina, what did May say?"*

*Melina: "She said she wanted to play soccer and I wouldn't let her. But there were too many kids playing already."*

*Teacher: "I know you would like to answer what May is saying, Melina. And you'll get your turn in a few minutes. But right now, try very hard to just tell May exactly what you heard her say."*

*Melina: "She said that she wanted to play soccer but I wouldn't let her because there were too many people. I made her mad and I guess it made her feel that we thought there was something wrong with her."*

*Teacher: "Is that pretty accurate May?"*

*May: "She forgot the part about me not being good enough to play."*

*Teacher: "Melina?"*

*Melina: "OK. I told her there were too many people and that she wasn't good enough."*

*Teacher: "Was that more or less what you meant, May?"*

*May: "Yeah, it is. I'm glad she heard me."*

*Teacher: "Good. Now it's Melina's turn. You listen and then tell her what she said."*

*Melina: "Every time we play there are always too many people. It spoils the game, so we decided that no more than 10 kids could play on each side. When May showed up we already had that. It's not that we don't like her, we just had too many people. I'm sorry I said she wasn't good enough."*

*Teacher: "Good. OK May, what did Melina say?"*

*May:* "She said that there were too many kids so they came up with a rule. She said it wasn't that they didn't like me. But, I didn't have a say in that rule. It's not fair."

*Teacher:* "We'll talk about what would be a fair way to figure out how many kids can play at once in a second, but what did Melina say about how she felt about you?"

*May:* "She said she didn't want the game to be spoiled and she was sorry she said a mean thing about me."

*Melina:* "That's right."

Although it wasn't easy, both girls feel relieved that they were finally heard, and even better, understood. They heard each other because the pace of the discussion was slowed right down. That's a very important point. When someone's emotion is up, as it usually is when there is an argument or difference of opinion, it makes them hard of hearing. The communication is all one-way. Having to wait and listen to the other person, especially closely enough so that you can actually repeat what they said and then report on how they were feeling, gives everyone a chance to cool off and slow down. It allows the interaction to resemble a civilized conversation – an all-too-rare occurrence these days. The sad fact is that most people have never learned how to listen, really listen, to others. The class meeting is a perfect opportunity to correct this rather large social flaw. Think of how many human-interaction problems could be solved just by the sharpening of this one skill.

Once Melina and May have spoken and heard each other, it's time for the class to work together to come up with a solution. In this case, there is obviously a problem with too many soccer players and not enough soccer games. As with most problems dealt with in the class meeting, ask for suggestions from the group. This not only gets everyone else involved, but takes the focus off of May and Melina so that it's no longer their problem (that is, a problem they have with each other) but something the entire class is working on.

Start by asking for suggestions (or, if you have progressed to the point where a student is chairing the meeting, have the chair call for suggestions). This is called brainstorming – everyone just calls out whatever comes into their heads, with no idea being too stupid or far-fetched. Yes, this will get a little chaotic at times, but that's part of the fun and also the creative part of the process. Write all the suggestions on a blackboard and vote on each one. You will probably have one or two good suggestions that nobody vetoes.

## More "points of view" exercises:

- Have one person recite a simple story: "I decided to make a chocolate cake. I knew I needed to buy four eggs, two cups of sugar, and a package of chocolate. I went to the store. But when I came home I couldn't make the cake because I had only bought three eggs and I completely forgot to buy the sugar. Boy, was I mad at myself." Someone else has to listen to the story and recite it back, including what the person's feelings were.
- Play the class some music or show them a photograph or a painting. Ask them to write down and then read aloud what they heard or saw and how it made them feel. This is a good exercise to show how different things affect people in different ways. Emphasize that there is no right or wrong way to look at a picture.
- Show them one of those pictures that can be seen in more than one way. The picture that can look like an ornate vase or the profile of a woman's face is a familiar one. You can also point out that people in Western cultures see a "man in the moon," while people in Eastern cultures often see a "rabbit in the moon". This is just another way to illustrate how perfectly valid different interpretations can be.
- Role Playing. This simple and enjoyable exercise takes advantage of children's natural flair for the dramatic. Essentially, when there is a problem between two or more

people, others in the class take their roles and act out the scenario. Do it once with a made-up problem so they get the idea before a real problem crops up.

Let's say Ronnie has been pestering a few of his friends during class, mainly just to get their attention. Someone plays Ronnie and others (not those involved) play his friends as they act out the scene. Ronnie could play one of his friends so he can experience first hand how his pestering affects them.

Once the scene has been acted out, the group can try and figure out why he is behaving this way, while the players can explain how they feel. Next, everyone tries to figure out a way it could have been done differently. For instance, if the group decides that Ronnie wants them to pay attention to him, they can suggest ways he could do it in a more helpful, non-disruptive way, like offering to help with their homework.

# CHAPTER 15

# Sociometry

I t's the first day of the new school year. As a teacher, you're naturally excited. But sometimes you wonder what kind of problems you might have with your new class. Worrying that you might not be able to fully cope with these potential problems can cause tension and anxiety. At the very least you wonder what attitudes and competencies these students will bring to the class, and how this will affect their relationship with each other and with you. Will they be friendly, helpful, cooperative, or hostile, aggressive, and a discipline problem? And will you be able to handle all of the problems that arise from the complex interactions of 20 or 30 young people thrown together with an adult, day after day?

In order to have a cooperative, well-disciplined class you need certain ingredients. Perhaps most the important is that each member of the class feel they belong to the group. They should feel accepted by the other students, confident about their own capacity for getting along with others, and able to develop their social interest. When any of these factors are not present, you're not going to have a harmonious classroom. Knowing how your students feel about each other gives you a special insight into how to prevent potential problems. Fortunately, there is a unique and eminently useful tool for understanding the group dynamics of these complex relationships from very early on, knowledge that can move your new class towards being an efficient and cooperative group. This tool is called sociometry. It is the science of understanding group dynamics, and more specifically, how individual students view each other; the likes and dislikes, animosities, friendships, and even ambivalence that exist in every class.

Sociometry is a systematic way of identifying the interaction patterns of students in the classroom. It helps the teacher understand the preferences that students have towards others in different situations, such as seating, committees, class projects, play, work, homework, as well as other forms of interaction. With this information, the teacher is in a position to evaluate what impact these relationships have on the social and academic development of the students. This sociometric evaluation makes it possible to enhance these relationships, to help everyone get along better, and therefore learn better.

At the root of sociometry is the fact that the classroom atmosphere is influenced by the social relationships of the students. If the class is socially dysfunctional, the withdrawn students will become more withdrawn, the defiant ones more defiant. Knowing how to diagnose the four goals of misbehavior (chapter 5) is important, but so is understanding the audience the child is playing up to, as well as the child's status in the group. In other words, the teacher has to concern herself not only with an individual student, but how that individual student is seen by the whole group and even the subgroups existing in the class.

The tool of Sociometry allows the teacher to understand the structure of these social relationships and therefore change and influence them in a way that can bring greater harmony to the classroom atmosphere.

## Sociometric tests

The sociometric test is designed to help the teacher learn how individual students are perceived by their peers. It consists of a simple questionnaire that each student fills out. The bulk of the sociometric questionnaire consists of asking students to choose the classmates they would prefer to sit with or do things with.

Don't call it a test (that gives the impression there are right or wrong answers), call it a survey or questionnaire. It's important to be very casual when introducing it. Tell them what it's for and how it will be done. Make it very clear that complete confidentiality will be observed. This is crucial for the success of the test for the obvious reason that few of us want our intimate preferences known.

Since you will want to repeat this test at intervals throughout the year, utilize the information gained immediately so that the students see the purpose of the testing.

Your explanation of the test can go something like this:

"Soon, we're going to come up with our seating arrangement for the class. I would like to know which people you would prefer to sit near."

Make it clear that if they do not get their first choice, they will be able to have their second or third choice. Tell them: "The choices you make are private and I will be the only one who reads your responses."

After handing out the questionnaire (see page 194), ask the class to write the names of their first choice, second choice, and third choice for the seating arrangement. If there is someone that they really don't want to sit near, they should put that name in the place that is indicated, otherwise they should leave that space blank."

Almost any activity that requires group participation is an opportunity for your students to make choices. Here are some examples of questions you can include in your questionnaire:

## At school

- ✎ Who would you like to work with on committees, projects, bulletin boards or homework?
- ✎ Who would you like to work with to help each other in math, spelling, science, French, social studies, etc.?

## On the playground

✎ Who would you like to have on your team? As team captain? To play with?

## At home

✎ Who would you like to invite to a party? Sleep over with? Go to a movie with? Walk home with?

# The Sociometry Questionnaire Form

Name _____

Date _____

A. Pick three people you would like to sit near in class:
1st Choice _____
2nd Choice _____
3rd Choice _____

I would prefer not to sit near (*You don't have to answer this if you don't want to.*) _____

B. Pick three people you would like to play with the most at recess:
1st Choice _____
2nd Choice _____
3rd Choice _____

I would prefer not to play with (*You don't have to answer this if you don't want to.*) _____

C. Pick three people you would most want to work on a group project with:
1st Choice _____
2nd Choice _____
3rd Choice _____

I would prefer not to work in a group project with (*You don't have to answer this if you don't want to.*) _____

# Learning from the results of the sociometry test

## The stars

The students who are the most frequently chosen are called stars. They are called stars because their classmates tend to form around them the way planets form around stars (see sociogram chart, page 201). These classroom stars possess qualities that the others value and therefore want to associate with. Their characteristics can frequently be positive, but the star could also have qualities that bring great difficulties to the classroom.

These positive qualities could include being: friendly, accepting, good looking, encouraging, humorous, energetic, playful, fun, engaging, positive, optimistic, high achieving in sports, academics or games.

On the negative side, they may have been chosen because they are: strong, powerful, rebellious, mischievous, critical, tough, or even promiscuous.

Some choices are made because the children have similar values, interests, behavior patterns, race, religion, academic achievement, sports, gender, or simply because they live near one another.

These different attributes, all of which can be seen as desirable at one time or another by different students, explains why some children can be chosen because they are cooperative and others chosen because they are uncooperative.

The stars who are chosen because they don't cooperate with the teacher can have a detrimental impact on the classroom atmosphere. Students who are popular because of their rebellion or attention-getting behaviors can be a nightmare because the class actually encourages their negative behavior.

In order to help these popular rebels redirect their energies from destructive to constructive behavior, it helps to know how well they are liked and by whom. Sometimes a student having leadership qualities is capable of creating greater negative influence on the classroom's environment than the teacher can exert in a positive way.

## The fringe students

Students who are only chosen by one other student are called fringe students. They are on the outer edge of the group, and have only one other person in the group they feel close to. They don't feel important to others in the group, and the people they would prefer to be with often don't choose them as their primary choice. These students may find it difficult to fit in, and could give up trying to form better friendships. They may even try to find their sense of belonging or significance through any of the four goals of misbehavior.

## The isolates

The child who is never chosen by any of the students in the classroom is called an isolate. This child does not have any one in the group seeking her out, so the feeling of belonging is not there. They may find their place in the group by attention getting or rebellion, which can ostracize them even further, but at least this gives them a presence, where otherwise (without the acting-out behavior) they could be invisible. Other "isolates" in the group are so discouraged and fearful of the other students that they would actually rather be invisible. Being anonymous allows them to move into their own world, to fantasize and not participate in every day social and academic activities. These children tend to be absent more frequently, may have somatic complaints stemming from stress, and may be depressed and unhappy. Their academic work could seriously suffer because they have no motivation to work. Sometimes students who arrive at school in midyear have great difficulty making friends and therefore feel very lonely and isolated.

## The rejected students

The students who are openly rejected (someone has specifically said they don't want to sit near or work with them) by the group are the ones who will suffer the most in this classroom. Their feelings are frequently hurt, and having no one to associate with, are left to delve deeper and deeper into their own world. Although they usually stick to themselves, such students could retaliate and become violent and dangerous if they are bullied, teased, or come from a difficult home situation.

# The sociogram

A sociogram is a diagram that graphically shows all of the attractions and rejections in the group. It depicts the social choices your students have made, and provides valuable clues as to their personal values, attitudes, and reasons for uncooperative behavior in the class. It gives the teacher an opportunity to determine each child's position in the group, as well as the role that each child would like to occupy. This allows you to analyze which students can play positive roles in respect to the class as a whole, and who can be of help to other students. For instance, the skillful placing of a fringe student with a more popular student may provide him with the status he needs in order to feel important and significant in the group. Poor friendship choices may hinder a child from improving, while arranging for better associations may help her to climb out of her difficulties. That is perhaps the most compelling reason why the sociogram is such an important tool for all teachers.

The sociometric test should be given to each child once a month for the first three months of the school year (starting after the first month) so that you can gauge the progress you are making in helping children find more suitable relationships within the group. After that, you can give them once every other month to keep tabs on these relationships.

It's important to test your class on a regular basis because these all-important classroom relationships can change. You may start the year with a very cooperative class, only to have problems surface after a few months due to something as simple as a few changes in friendships, resulting in a change in the dynamics of the class. Periodic sociometry tests help you fine-tune the groupings.

Other things to look for in difficult relationships:

- Relationships that are formed due to cultural, racial, or religious affiliations, often as a result of prejudices or mis-understandings between different groups within the class. It is important to help these children understand that our humanness means that we have most things in common, with only slight, cosmetic differences because of our culture, etc. In multicultural groups it's important for children to learn about cultural differences, as well as the real reasons for differences in things like clothing, diet, and rituals. Learning about others helps to alleviate the mystery. Group discussions about our differences help children realize that others have the same problems, doubts, and fears as they do.

- Children struggling for power in the classroom can lead to rivalry, bullying, and violence both inside and outside of school.

- Competition for excellence can lead to struggles between individuals, which can manifest in criticism, fault-finding, and negativism. Relationships can suffer when people look down on others from a superior position. They then look for allies to support their view. Opposition groups form and then the different groups struggle against each other. This can readily be seen in the war that regularly goes on between boys and girls, especially in the early years. Just listen to how children talk about the opposite sex. The boys complain that the girls act like they are perfect, while the boys are bad. This inter-gender conflict may appear to be just a part of growing up, but make no mistake, it can lead to problems. Boys and girls can and should learn to be friends with each other. These issues have to be worked out together during class discussion.

✎ Physically weak children who select physically strong children may have feelings of inferiority and are looking for someone to protect them. Conversely, when physically strong children select small, less powerful children as friends, it may indicate that they like to control others or feel superior by associating with weaker children. Of course these selections could be made for reasons not connected to being strong or weak, but just because they are good friends.

✎ If a troublemaker is selected by most of the children, it may be due to the fact that others are vicariously living through this acting-out child because they are too afraid to act out themselves. With children who live vicariously, this acting out behavior may come at a later time, when they finally achieve the courage to act out their inner rebellious feelings.

✎ When an attention-getting child is selected as the star in the classroom, her status in the class may stem from her misbehavior. That means her classmates are encouraging it, so you can bet it will continue unless you do something about it. On the other hand, if the attention getting child is an isolate, she may feel that no one will pay attention to her unless she does act up. Her behavior may be the only way she has found to get at least some kind of attention from the others in her class.

✎ The child who is rejected by the class may become vicious, hurtful, or try to get revenge by name-calling and put-downs. The rejected child may be so hurt by the others in the class, that he feels the only way to defend himself is to be offensive. This one child may have a powerful influence on the class simply because he is so difficult. He is an ever-present threat and therefore the children want to hurt him back. If this is not dealt with, the class could suffer immeasurable harm.

✎ The child who rejects others has a very strong negative feeling about them. This kind of child is very judgmental and their negative feelings may be expressed as unfriendliness or through put-down behavior. This is why it is so important not to put rejected people together.

By using the following sociometric test in conjunction with class discussions, you will be in a position to help all of these children form healthy and helpful relationships.

The example (right) of a sociometric matrix is designed to help you chart the status of each student in your class, as well as the complex group dynamics that are constantly evolving and changing. Make a blank matrix chart so that you can record the results after each monthly or bimonthly test. You will need this information in order to complete the diagram on page 203. You can also use this chart to track and help improve the relationships in your classroom. In other words, the chart is the raw data and the diagram is the visual aid. Both will help you:

✎ improve the group dynamics of your class (and therefore academic performance);

✎ help your students overcome relationship problems;

✎ draw up seating arrangements

✎ access the social skills that each child has or lacks

# Sociometric Matrix

| Chosen → / Chooser ↓ | Alice | Betty | Carol | Dawn | Fran | Gail | Helen | Joyce | Kelly | Mary | Nancy | Pat | Sara | Alan | Bob | Cal | Dick | Fred | John | Mike |
|---|---|---|---|---|---|---|---|---|---|---|---|---|---|---|---|---|---|---|---|---|
| **Total** | 0 | 18 | 3 | 2 | 8 | 12 | 0 | -6 | 16 | 5 | 1 | 13 | 1 | 7 | 5 | 1 | 12 | 2 | -4 | 14 |
| Alice |  | 1 |  |  | 3 | 2 |  | R |  |  |  |  |  |  |  |  |  |  | R |  |
| Betty |  |  |  |  |  | 2 |  |  | 1 |  |  | . |  | 3 |  |  |  |  |  |  |
| Carol |  | 1 |  | 2 |  | 3 |  |  |  |  |  |  |  |  |  |  |  |  | R |  |
| Dawn |  | 3 | 1 |  |  |  |  | R |  |  |  | 2 |  |  |  |  |  |  |  |  |
| Fran |  |  |  |  |  | 2 |  | R |  |  |  | 1 |  |  |  |  | 3 |  |  |  |
| Gail |  | 3 |  |  | 1 |  |  | R | 2 |  |  |  |  |  |  |  |  |  |  |  |
| Helen |  |  |  |  |  |  |  |  | 1 | 3 |  | 2 |  |  |  |  |  |  |  |  |
| Joyce |  | 1 |  |  |  |  |  |  | 2 | 3 |  |  |  |  |  |  |  |  | R |  |
| Kelly |  | 1 |  |  |  | 2 |  |  |  | 3 |  |  |  |  |  |  |  |  |  |  |
| Mary |  |  |  |  |  |  |  |  | 1 |  | 3 | 2 |  |  |  |  |  |  |  |  |
| Nancy |  |  |  |  |  |  |  |  | 1 | 2 |  | 3 |  |  |  |  |  |  |  |  |
| Pat |  |  |  |  | 1 | 2 |  |  |  |  |  |  | 3 |  |  |  |  |  |  |  |
| Sara |  | 2 |  |  |  | 3 |  |  |  |  |  | 1 |  |  |  |  |  |  |  |  |
| Alan |  |  |  |  |  |  |  |  |  |  |  |  |  |  | 2 | 3 | 1 |  |  |  |
| Bob |  |  |  |  |  |  |  |  |  |  |  |  |  | 2 |  |  |  | 3 |  | 1 |
| Cal |  |  |  |  |  |  |  | R |  |  |  |  |  | 2 |  |  |  | 3 |  | 1 |
| Dick |  |  |  | 3 |  |  |  |  |  |  |  |  |  | 2 |  |  |  |  |  | 1 |
| Fred |  |  |  |  |  |  |  | R |  |  |  |  |  | 3 |  | 2 |  |  | R | 1 |
| John |  |  |  |  |  |  |  |  |  |  |  |  |  | 3 |  |  | 1 |  |  | 2 |
| Mike |  | 2 |  |  |  |  |  |  |  |  |  |  |  | 3 |  |  | 1 |  |  |  |
| 1st = (3) |  | 4 | 1 |  | 2 |  |  |  | 4 |  |  | 2 |  |  |  |  | 3 |  |  | 4 |
| 2nd = (2) |  | 2 |  | 1 |  | 5 |  |  | 2 | 1 |  | 3 |  | 2 | 2 |  | 1 |  |  | 1 |
| 3rd = (1) |  | 2 |  |  | 2 | 2 |  |  |  | 3 | 1 | 1 | 1 | 3 | 1 | 1 | 1 | 2 |  |  |
| Rejections |  |  |  |  |  |  |  | 6 |  |  |  |  |  |  |  |  |  |  | 4 |  |
| **Total** | 0 | 18 | 3 | 2 | 8 | 12 | 0 | -6 | 16 | 5 | 1 | 13 | 1 | 7 | 5 | 1 | 12 | 2 | -4 | 14 |
| **Stars** |  | + |  |  |  | + |  |  | + |  |  | + |  |  |  |  | + |  |  | + |
| **Average** |  |  | + | + |  |  |  |  |  | + |  |  |  | + | + |  |  |  |  |  |
| **Isolates** | + |  |  |  |  |  | + |  |  |  |  |  |  |  |  |  |  |  |  |  |
| **Fringe** |  |  |  | + |  |  |  |  |  |  |  | + | + |  |  |  | + | + |  |  |
| **Rejected** |  |  |  |  |  |  |  | + |  |  |  |  |  |  |  |  |  |  | + |  |

# The Sociometric Diagram – visualizing the group dynamics of your class

The squares represent the boys in the class and the circles the girls. If you follow the arrows connecting each student, you can see whom each child chose to be with and, in some cases, whom they chose to not be with.

A line with two strokes through it represents a mutual choice (two children have chosen each other).

A broken (dotted) line indicates a child choosing someone from the opposite sex.

The number beside the arrowhead indicates the order of preference – how this child has been chosen or rejected by another person (a "0" means the person was rejected by someone, a "1" indicates a first choice, and so on).

The numbers inside the squares or circles indicates the total number of positive or negative points that child received. Being someone's first choice gives that student 3 points, a second choice gives them 2 points, a third choice is 1, not being chosen by anyone is a 0 and being rejected is a –1. For example, from the above diagram we can see that Carol chose Betty as her first choice (although Betty didn't choose Carol). Carol chose Dawn as her second choice, a mutual attraction since Dawn chose Carol as her first choice. Carol also rejected John (one of many who rejected him).

As you can see, it's best to put the stars in the middle of the diagram (after all, the social aspect of the class does seem to revolve around them), and the isolates and the fringe students on the outside.

## Sociometric Matrix analysis

Generally speaking, the imaginary fifth grade class we have depicted on page 203 is probably experiencing a lot of difficulty, both academically and behaviorally.

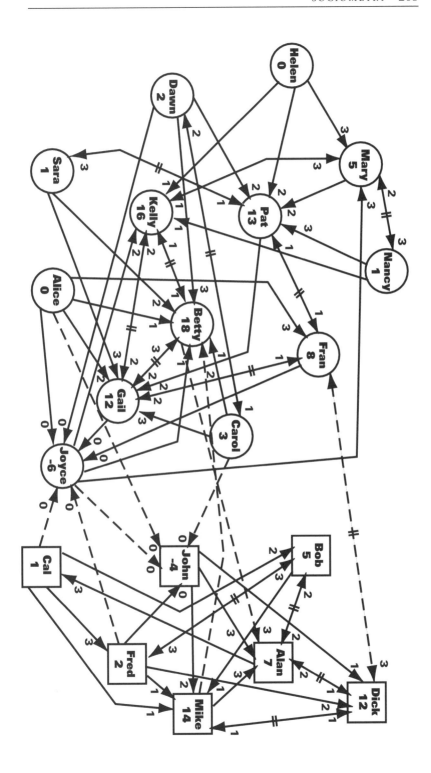

When we study the relationships in this class, we observe that there are two students, a boy and a girl, who are rejected by almost 25% of the other students. The behavior from the other students that demonstrates this behavior could be in the form of put-downs, threats, or ignoring. More than likely, these two students are experiencing hurt feelings. (If the animosity between students erupts into open battle, there could be a lot of fighting and perhaps gangs or cliques formed.)

Four girls have rejected John, so we can guess that John's relationships with girls is not so great, and this may even include his relationship with his teacher if she is a woman. Two out of the seven boys reject Joyce, while four girls also reject her. This indicates that she not only has difficulty with boys but also with girls. Because of the lines of friendships existing in this class, Joyce will have a very difficult time being accepted by any group except one. John is not as frequently rejected by the boys as he is by the girls, which could indicate that he will be able to be integrated into a group of boys more easily than Joyce.

Another problem in the class is that there are two children who are isolates, that is, they don't have any students interested in being with them. This may be because they have poor social skills, and they may therefore need to be with a popular student so they can model methods of interacting with others successfully. The isolates could achieve some much-needed status by being seen associating with socially successful students. It's also important to assess why these isolates have not been chosen. If they are not chosen because they are withdrawn, passive, or shy, then they should be put into small groups of between three to five students. This will encourage them to participate more because they can't easily withdraw in a small group. These children will not feel they belong to the class and may daydream in order to go elsewhere, anywhere other than in the group. If their isolation is allowed to continue, they may have greater feelings of inadequacy, which could effect their academic work. The others in the class could end up teasing them, which could result in an increase in absences. Of course, if this is a new class and the students don't know them at all, it's possible that integration will be quicker.

There are five students who are on the fringe: Cal, Sara, Dawn, Nancy and Carol. That means that only one student chose them. They do not have strong attachments but three of them (Dawn, Carol and Nancy) have a mutual choice with one other child in the class. This would indicate there is a good chance for them to make additional friends if they are sitting near or working with their choices in small groups.

The stars are extremely important in uniting the group because they have the power to bring status and importance to the students who lack good relations with others. Although you must give the rejected children and the isolates their first choices, it's not important for the stars to get their first choice since they have no difficulty in getting along with others.

There are six stars in the class: Mike, Dick, Gail, Betty, Kelly and Pat. If any of these stars are antagonistic to the teacher or rebellious in any way, you can count on having severe discipline problems. That's because the stars are leaders and are therefore capable of leading the class against you. It's important to move the stars toward cooperation by giving them responsibility and by allowing them to play a leadership role in the classroom. Giving them opportunity to help others is one way of creating a feeling of social interest within them. Of course, if these stars are already cooperative, then you have allies and are in a very good position to solve your discipline problems much faster and with more ease.

## Groupings

After assessing which children are having difficulty in their relationships with others, we can start arranging the groups. (Keep in mind that your class will need lots of activities where the children get to know each other better.)

The grouping of Dawn, Carol, Fran, and Gail is the most difficult. Although they have well-established lines of communication between them, they all reject Joyce. Through their interaction with each other they can continue to put Joyce in a bad light and therefore should be broken up wherever possible.

Here are the recommended groupings for this fifth grade class:

*Groups*

| 1 | 2 | 3 | 4 | 5 |
|---|---|---|---|---|
| Joyce | Betty | Pat | Mike | Alan |
| Kelly | Alice | Fran | Dick | Fred |
| Mary | Gail | Dawn | Cal | Bob |
| Nancy | Carol | Sara | John | Helen |

### Group 1

Joyce was given her 2nd and 3rd choices.

Normally we would want to put Joyce with her 1st choice but couldn't because Betty was already grouped with two girls (Alice and Gail) who rejected Joyce.

### Group 2

Alice, whom no one chose, was given her 1st choice, Betty. We could not put Joyce with her 1st choice, Betty, because Alice and Gail rejected Joyce.

Helen, an isolate, was given her 1st choice, Kelly, and her 3rd choice, Mary.

Group one may have the most difficulty cooperating because of Joyce, but Mary and Kelly are stars chosen by Joyce, and are also both mutual choices who did not reject anyone on the questionnaire.

Betty had the most choices. Alice, an isolate, and Carol, a fringe, both chose Betty as their 1st choice, so they should have their preferences given to them. Betty and Gail are mutual choices.

*Group 3*

In group three, Pat and Fran need to help Dawn and Sara who are on the fringe of the class. Through a process of elimination they had to be placed in this group because Fran has strong feelings against John and Joyce.

*Group 4*

In Group four, Mike and Dick will help John by modeling appropriate behavior. Being with Mike and Dick, the most popular of the boys, can help John gain some status. Cal, who is on the fringe in the class, chose Mike and Dick as his 1st and 2nd choice, therefore it was also important to have him in this group.

*Group 5*

Alan and Bob mutually chose each other, and Fred and Bob mutually chose each other, therefore this group should get along well.

## Student profile

Student profiles are a valuable tool in the study of the students in the classroom. The profiles provide information about the student's own views about themselves, authority figures, family members, siblings, their school, academic work, etc., which helps the teacher to plan a strategy for helping the student.

## Autobiography

Student's full name _____

Date _____

1. Brothers' names and ages: _____

_____

2. Sisters' names and ages

_____

3. What do you most enjoy doing?

_____

4. Name some of your best friends.

_____

5. What do you enjoy doing with your friends?

_____

6. List all of your interests

_____

_____

_____

_____

7. If you take special lessons, list them.

_____

8. Are there any special lessons you would like to take?

_____

9. What are your favorite TV programs?

_____

10. If you could be any other person, who would you be?

_____

Why?

_____

11. What kind of work would you like to do when you become an adult?

_____

Why?

_____

12. If you had to pretend that you were an animal, what animal would you choose to be?

_____

What qualities does this animal have that you like?

_____

13. Name some of your hobbies

_____

14. What are your favorite subjects in school?

_____

15. What subject do you like the least?

_____

Why?

_____

16. What do you like best about school?

_____

17. What do you like least about school?

_____

Why?

_____

18. If you could have any three wishes, what would they be?

_____

Why?

_____

Wish One

_____

Wish Two

_____

Wish Three

_____

19. What are some of the things that you are most afraid of?

_____

20. What is your favorite movie?

_____

## Your Thoughts About

Complete the following:

1. I...

_____

2. My family

_____

3. Friends

_____

4. I always

_____

5. I never

_____

6. What I like best about myself is

_____

7. What I need to improve in is

_____

8. I want

_____

9. I believe

_____

10. I must

_____

11. I should

_____

12. I fear

_____

13. Kids are always

_____

14. Kids never

_____

15. My family is always

_____

16. My mother

_____

17. My father

_____

18. What I enjoy most about my friends are

_____

19. What I like least about my friends are

_____

20. I wish my friends would

_____

21. My siblings never

_____

Having a student complete these sentences is one of the best ways to discover their feelings about themselves and others. It allows them free rein to express their unique ways of looking at personal problems, as well as their private logic. It also gives you an opportunity to glean some valuable insights into your students' personalities. These views can be assessed again in a few months to see if their convictions have changed. This is an excellent way for the teacher to assess the progress she has been making in her effort to have the students become more cooperative. The above survey, applicable to grade 3 and up to high school, can be given during the second week, after students get to know each other.

# References

Ansbacher, H. and Ansbacher, R., *The Individual Psychology of Alfred Adler.* New York: Harper and Row, 1956.

Canfield, J., and Wells, H.C. *100 Ways to Enhance Self-Concept in the Classroom.* New Jersey: Prentice-Hall, 1976.

Combs, A. and Snygg, D., *Individual Behavior.* New York: Harper and Bros.

Coopersmith, S., *The Antecedents of Self-Esteem.* San Francisco: W. H. Freeeman, 1967.

Corsini, R., and Howard, D., *Critical Incidents in Teaching.* New Jersey: Prentice-Hall, 1964.

Dinkmeyer, D. and Caldwell, E., *Developmental Counseling and Guidance: A Comprehensive School Approach.* New York: McGraw-Hill, 1970.

Dinkmeyer, D. and Losoncy, L. *The Encouragement Book.* New York: Prentice-Hall, 1980.

Dreikurs, R., *Character Education and Spiritual Values in an Anxious Age.* Chicago: Alfred Adler Institute, 1952.

Dreikurs, R., *Challenge of Parenthood.* New York: Duell, Sloan, and Pearce, 1958.

Dreikurs, R., and Cassel, P., *Discipline Without Tears.* Toronto: Prentice-Hall, 1974.

Dreikurs, R., Grunwald, B., and Pepper, F., *Maintaining Sanity in the Classroom.* New York: Harper and Row, 1982.

Dreikurs, R., *Psychology in the Classroom.* New York: Harper and Row, 1957.

Faber, A ., and Mazlish, E., *How to Talk so Kids Will Listen & Listen so Kids will Talk.* Avon, York, 1982.

Glasser, W., *Schools Without Failure.* New York: Harper and Row, 1969.

Goleman, D., *Emotional Intelligence.* New York: Bantam Books, 1994.

Manaster, G., and Corsini, R., *Individual Psychology.* United States: Peacock, 1982.

Maslow, A., *Motivation and Personality.* New York: Harper and Row, 1970.

McKay, M., and Fanning, P., *Self-Esteem.* Oakland: New Harbinger, 1987.

Nelson, J., Lott, L., and Glenn, S., *Positive Discipline in the Classroom.* Prima, Rocklin, CA, 1997.

Olweus, D., *Bullying at School: What We Know and What We Can Do.* Oxford, UK: Blackwell, 1993.

Shapiro, S., and Skinulis, K., *Parent Talk.* Toronto: Stoddart, 1997.

Shapiro, S., Skinulis, K., and Skinulis, R., *Practical Parenting.* Toronto: Practical Parenting Program, 1996.

Purkey, W., *Self-Concept and School Achievement.* New Jersey: Prentice-Hall, 1970.

Spiel, O., *Discipline Without Punishment.* London: Faber and Faber, 1962.

# INDEX